Praise for *Winging It*

"Emma is one of the smartest and most impressive entrepreneurs I've ever met. In *Winging It*, she distills her ideas about business, life, and relationships into principles that anyone can apply to improve upon their own lives."

MARK MANSON
author of *The Subtle Art of Not Giving a F*ck* and *Everything Is F*cked*

"Emma is an entrepreneur who has stayed the course and created an overnight success story that's been over twenty years in the making. She has proven that patience, persistence, and the way you treat people are critical elements in running a thriving company. *Winging It* is the culmination of the past two decades' worth of experiences and deserves a wide audience. Bravo!"

ALLI WEBB
cofounder of Drybar

"*Winging It* will show you how to map out what's important to you, stay focused on achieving your goals, and thrive."

ARIANNA HUFFINGTON
founder of *HuffPost* and Thrive Global

"Emma Isaacs is a true force of nature and a role model all women can learn from."

DIANE VON FURSTENBERG
founder of Diane von Furstenberg

"*Winging It* stands high above the other 'self-help' books of this era. Emma Isaacs is no lightweight. This book is rife with profound thinking and common-sense solutions to all the business and personal hurdles we all face on a daily basis. Bravo to Emma and *Winging It*, a courageous and comprehensive blueprint for striving toward our potential in every aspect of our lives."

DIANA NYAD
author, journalist, motivational speaker, long-distance swimmer

"Emma didn't invent women. She just showed up to lead them."

SETH GODIN
entrepreneur, bestselling author, speaker

"As any entrepreneur will tell you, the path to success is winding and never linear. To succeed takes tremendous grit, a great deal of smarts, and a lot of sacrifice too. It takes asking for help, building your network, and getting up more times than you fall. What's unique about Emma's story is that she's an entrepreneur through and through—someone who has never worked for anybody else and has had to figure out how to scale and build momentum without always having the answers to guide her. *Winging It* is an inspiring and practical resource for anyone looking to get ahead and master the game of entrepreneurship."

MARC RANDOLPH
author, cofounder and first CEO of Netflix

"Emma's energy and enthusiasm for business shine brightly."

SIR RICHARD BRANSON
founder of Virgin Group

"Emma Isaacs has created an ongoing forum to allow women's voices to be heard. She has championed the empowerment of women for many years and will continue to be an innovator and disruptor for years to come."

DEBORRA-LEE FURNESS
actor, director, activist

"Throughout my entire career, I was winging it all along! I never had a clue how to do it all until I did, and now I know I'm not alone. Emma doesn't just make it all look so easy—she charges into her life as a great big adventure, and we can't help but jump in too! Her energy is contagious, her optimism infectious, and her 'no holds barred' bravery makes us all determined to *never* shrink ourselves no matter what the odds are."

JANE WURWAND
cofounder of Dermalogica

"More vital than ever are people who have found the courage to forge their independence and find power on their own terms. Emma is a strong example of a woman who is willing to step out of comfort to be a role model for others, and ultimately show us that whatever we're seeking is possible if we believe it to be so."

ALYSSA MILANO
actor, producer, activist

"Emma is the type of person who just makes things happen. Every one of us can learn something from the way she conducts herself and her attitude toward life and business."

KATE HUDSON
actor and cofounder of Fabletics

"*Winging It* is the call to arms we all need. It's the encouragement we seek and the reassurance we crave to truly step forward, arms outstretched, and ask for what we want."

AMY CUDDY, PHD
social psychologist, Harvard University executive
education teacher, bestselling author of *Presence*

"Now more than ever we need to hear the voices of strong female role models in every aspect of society. Emma Isaacs's visionary leadership has provided a platform for those voices in communities around the globe. Her work empowering women personifies influence in action and models the way for stepping into your own leadership zone with courage and confidence."

LOIS FRANKEL, PHD
New York Times bestselling author of *Nice Girls Don't Get the
Corner Office*, president of Corporate Coaching International

"A lot of people put pressure on themselves to do everything well every day—be an amazing friend, be great at their job, be a supportive spouse, and be a perfect parent. But my philosophy has been more about giving yourself permission to be 'well-lopsided,' and Emma is a person who lives and breathes that philosophy. She's a role model and guiding light for anyone wanting to achieve similar success in business and life, and *Winging It* is a manual to get you there!"

RANDI ZUCKERBERG
founder and CEO of Zuckerberg Media

"Emma Isaacs is a BOSS. And she is a delight. She is kind, and she is smart, and she is grounded, and she is brave and funny."

ELIZABETH GILBERT
author of *Eat Pray Love*

WINGING IT

stop thinking *start doing*

WHY ACTION BEATS PLANNING EVERY TIME

EMMA ISAACS

sounds true
BOULDER, COLORADO

Sounds True
Boulder, CO 80306

Published 2020

Book design by Linsey Dodaro

Printed in South Korea

Library of Congress Cataloging-in-Publication Data

Names: Isaacs, Emma, 1979- author.
Title: Winging it: stop thinking, start doing : why action beats planning
 every time / Emma Isaacs.
Description: Boulder, CO : Sounds True, 2020.
Identifiers: LCCN 2019055969 (print) | LCCN 2019055970 (ebook) | ISBN
 9781683646907 (hardback) | ISBN 9781683646914 (ebook)
Subjects: LCSH: Success. | Self-actualization (Psychology)
Classification: LCC BF637.S8 I83 2020 (print) | LCC BF637.S8 (ebook) |
 DDC 158.1--dc23
LC record available at https://lccn.loc.gov/2019055969
LC ebook record available at https://lccn.loc.gov/2019055970

10 9 8 7 6 5 4 3 2 1

CONTENTS

THIS BOOK IS FOR YOU

This book is for you if, like me, you've always felt a little bit restless and curious, like there might be something more out there for you. It's for you if you want to learn a bunch of shortcuts about how to start your own company, grow your business, become a more valued employee, build wealth, find more time, or just pack more living into every day.

Since before I can remember, I've been seeking a big life full of adventure, and that has manifested in what I have today: a global business making life better for women, and a crazy household that lets our six little humans flourish and fail.

I dropped out of university and began starting my own companies at a very early age. That means I'm largely self-taught and self-made, guided only by the simple values my parents taught me: be kind always, smile and laugh as much as possible, and give as much as you can. So far, it's served me, my businesses, and my family well.

I've never been someone who has sought balance. The idea of having your life in perfect equilibrium has always felt a little unattainable and elusive to me. I just try to bring more health and sanity into my life where I can, never attempting to have the scales tipped perfectly each day. It's completely unrealistic to think you can work out; grow your own vegetables; run an empire; be a great partner, mother, and friend, as well as an infallible leader; and also give time and energy to the causes you value. With a global business, an unrelenting travel schedule, and young children, that's just not possible for me right now.

Your life doesn't need to look anything like mine. Perhaps you've made a choice not to have a business or not to have a family. Just because

I've made these choices doesn't mean I believe everyone should follow in the same way.

What I do believe is that we can fall into the habit of thinking we're not good enough or smart enough. We can also hide behind the excuse that it's just not the right time to do what we really want to do. We wait to be tapped on the shoulder. We wait for our circumstances to improve. We falter because we're afraid.

I want to be the friend who walks alongside you, saying, "Guess what? We made all that up in our heads." I know there's a path for you to take that will lead you to where you want to be. But that path ultimately starts with you—no one else can take that first step.

The most important work to do is on our mindsets and self-talk. It's easy to compare and despair, constantly looking outside of ourselves for validation. We have to stop thinking like this and instead, look inward and say, "What's my uniqueness? What's my gift to the world? How can I amplify that?"

I do what I do at Business Chicks because I want to be a light for other women. I want to show you that anything's possible, whether it be in business, with financial independence and success, philanthropy, or even childbirth. I started out with no qualifications in any of these areas and have been able to achieve what I set out to and more. I know you can too.

I do what I do because I want to lift women up and celebrate their achievements. I want to challenge thinking on issues and give people the confidence to back themselves, stand out, try something scary, build their wealth, make an impact, fail a lot, and get up and try again.

And why do I want that for others? Because, perhaps selfishly, it's what I want for myself.

I'm about to welcome you into my world. Show you what works for me and share openly what hasn't. I hope that what you find in the pages of this book inspires you to dream up new ways to be kind to people and to think about how the game you're currently playing might be worthy of a bigger court. I hope it stretches your thinking about what's possible, and shows you that when you take giant leaps of faith, the only challenging thing will be some temporary discomfort.

Are you ready?

LET'S DO THIS.

JUST
START

"It was 1989, and I was a fitness instructor. I had formal design knowledge, I was an average sewer, and I would spend my weekends sewing outfits to wear to class because I wanted something different—something I could wear to class and also wear in my everyday life! My students started asking where they could get activewear like mine, and then one day I found myself standing in front of my class and realized that everyone was wearing Lorna Jane. I remember thinking to myself, *You have to do this; you have to give it your all and see where it will take you.* I knew absolutely nothing about running a business, but the very next day I quit my day job and did it anyway. Today, we have more than 150 stores and are credited for inventing the activewear category."

LORNA JANE CLARKSON
founder, Lorna Jane

THE MAGIC OF WINGING IT

> The older you get, the more you realize that
> no one has a f***ing clue what they're doing.
> Everyone's just winging it.
>
> **UNKNOWN**

It's comforting to think that others have it all worked out and that successful people have a foolproof plan ready to whip out when things go wrong.

Here's the thing, though: no one really knows what they're doing.

No matter how much they're giving off the illusion of control and calm, at some level they're making it up as they go along, just like the rest of us.

Steve Jobs had never created a phone until Apple developed the iPhone. Ruth Bader Ginsburg had never been Associate Justice of the US Supreme Court before she started, and Arianna Huffington had never run a news organization before she pressed go on the *Huffington Post*.

A first-term president has never before been a president, and there's no greater example of making it up on the fly than being a first-time mom. You perform the ultimate act of "having a go" by pushing something the size of a watermelon out of an opening the size of a lemon and are then handed a little being you are responsible for and have no clue what to do with.

The realization that everyone is winging it is shocking at first, but once you've wrapped your head around the concept, it becomes deeply reassuring. Eventually, it can really set you free. Repeat after me: *I don't really know what I'm doing. Neither do you. We're all just making it up as we go along.*

When we give up the need to control everything and plan for every conceivable outcome, we create space for the unknown. When we don't have overly thought-out expectations of what's going to happen, we make room for surprises and allow ourselves to journey into uncharted territory. This is where we find growth.

A few years ago I had to fly across the country for a meeting, landing and departing on the same day. I'm always attempting three things at once, so when I arrived at the airport to pick up the rental car, I was on my phone with my laptop out trying to finish a pitch. When the woman finished the paperwork and handed over the keys, I mouthed my apologies for being so distracted and got on my way.

Still on the phone, it took me a good ten minutes to locate the car. A little hot and sweaty by now, I threw my bags in the back and jumped in the driver's seat, where something immediately felt not quite right. I glanced at the gearshift to my right. Aha! It was a manual car. I had no idea how to drive a manual car. By this time, I was running late for my meeting and was faced with two options: get my bags back out of the car, race back into the airport terminal, get even more hot and sweaty, stand in line, get a different car, and be desperately late to the one meeting I'd flown in for.

Or, I could wing it.

In a split second, I chose the latter.

Anyone else who was driving around that day would have seen a car bunny-hopping its way along the road, the driver cursing as she went. I cursed my parents for not insisting I learn to drive manual, I cursed the car companies for even inventing manual vehicles, and I cursed myself for thinking I could learn this skill on the fly.

After stalling several times at the traffic lights, with countless cars honking at me to get it together, I started to get the hang of it. And as I started to get the hang of it, my confidence grew. I started to thank my parents for never teaching me how to drive a manual car, I applauded the car companies for inventing such a cool vehicle, and most important, I praised myself for having the guts to think I could attempt something so bold.

Some of the best things to come from winging it are the stories you'll have to tell and the ways you'll be able to make others feel. I arrived at my meeting, smiling from ear to ear, confessing that I'd just taught myself to drive a manual car in the previous forty minutes. Of course, everyone thought I was a little bonkers, but I didn't care. I'd done it, and I felt on top of the world.

When you wing it, you learn how to trust yourself and develop more confidence. You start to believe that everything is going to be okay, and if not, at least you've felt something you've never felt before and you've tried something new. And that, my dear friend, could just about be the meaning of life right there.

Let me be clear: winging it is not the reckless absence of a plan. Nor is it the complete lack of skill. It's about not being so set in a plan that it prevents you from being led in different directions.

You should absolutely have a plan for your life, and for your business or career. But you should also give yourself the flexibility to pivot and weave when the situation calls for it.

WINGING IT means saying yes and working it out later.

WINGING IT means trying something before you think you're ready.

WINGING IT means less second-guessing yourself and more going with your gut.

WINGING IT means spending less time trying to concoct the perfect plan and future-proof yourself for dramas that probably won't eventuate.

WINGING IT means more time for going with the flow and celebrating the unexpected.

WINGING IT means getting comfortable with the uncomfortable.

WINGING IT allows you to try the thing you might hesitate to do if you had too much information.

WINGING IT is the act of believing in yourself enough to give your dreams a go.

WINGING IT puts you in control, and that's exactly where you deserve to be.

Brian Chesky, cofounder of Airbnb, once said, "I think you must always live and think like a child. Or have that childlike curiosity and wonder. That's probably the most important trait you can have, especially as an entrepreneur."

This way of thinking offers a beautiful alternative to living your life constantly comparing yourself to others and wondering if you're doing it right. Let's all get back to being more childlike, having fun, and being curious. Let's stress less and stop taking ourselves so seriously. Let's get back to experimenting and failing.

Let's get back to winging it.

NEVER READY

Nope, no way. There's no way I'm going to any event that calls themselves anything "chicks"!

ME

This is how I reacted when a friend invited me along to a networking event by a group called Business Chicks.

I was a twenty-four-year-old workaholic at the time, bulletproof and high on life. I was spending my days building my own recruitment agency, and was spending my nights . . . well, building my own recruitment agency.

The entrepreneurial bug had bitten me hard and, having dropped out of university, the world of business was now my classroom. In an attempt to school myself, I'd become something of a networking ninja, so I was genuinely surprised that my friend had managed to find a network that I wasn't already part of.

Appalled at the way it seemed to thrust an insult at women, I said to her, "That's a terrible name! I'm a serious entrepreneur!" She laughed and said, "Em, get over yourself. These events are amazing, and you're going to love it."

Thank heavens my friend was so convincing. I walked into that first Business Chicks event and was instantly uplifted by the space they'd created. I was used to having to psych myself up to deal with the boredom and beige of corporate networking events. Events I'd experienced before made me feel as though I'd have to put on my armor, go into battle, watch what I said, and appear to be someone I wasn't. I always left these things feeling a little bereft and wounded.

This event couldn't have made me feel any more different. The music was pumping and the women were smiling and happy. There was a level of possibility and positivity that I'd never seen before. There was a huge range of ages among the group, with women in the twilight years of their careers and women who were just starting out, and there was something binding them together that had nothing to do with their seniority or experience or even the industry they worked in. They were all there because they wanted to be—no manager or boss had made them, and the managers and bosses who had suggested they come along were probably getting gold stars later for being such awesome leaders.

I was seated in the back of the room, so far away from the stage that the speakers looked really small, but I couldn't have cared less. I loved the vibe of that room. All around me, I saw women greeting each other with hugs and listening intently to each other's stories. "So, this is what the sisterhood really looks like," I thought. "Sign me up!"

After that one event, I was hooked and on the biggest high. I became a member and signed all my staff members up too. Over the next few days, I shared my discovery with anyone who'd listen. I bought a bunch of tickets for the upcoming event and invited our clients and team members to come along with me.

At that next event, fate had its way with me. The marketing director of Business Chicks got up on stage to let the audience know that they were going to stop running the networking group, and that if there was anyone who might be interested in stepping in and taking over, she'd love to start a conversation with them.

Sitting next to me was Olivia Ruello, the general manager of my recruitment business, whose ambition and enthusiasm matched mine. At the time, Olivia and I worked so closely together that she could finish my sentences (and regularly did). As soon as the message was out of that marketing director's mouth, Liv leaned across and whispered in my ear, "You're going to buy it, aren't you?"

I smiled in return. "Yep!"

If you had looked at my situation at the time, you might have cautioned me to slow down. From the outside, there's no way I was "ready" to take on Business Chicks. In fact, I was advised by a lot of people not to even consider it. I had a good, strong business that was making money. We were growing healthfully, adding clients and people to the team at a steady pace; throwing a wrench in the works with a new business idea was probably not the thing we needed.

Here's the thing about entrepreneurs, though—cruising and coasting, even if it's profitable and stable, is not the speed we drive at.

I could see so much potential in the magic of what Business Chicks was and what it could be. There was a nagging voice in my head that said, "You'd be mad not to do this." The idea of bringing women together to learn, be uplifted, and belong to something really special was just too enticing.

At the time, I had no experience or knowledge of how to build a membership organization, nor had I ever run an event (unless my twenty-first birthday party counts), but what I lacked in experience, I made up for in determination and confidence. And sometimes, these are the only things you need to get going.

Too often, we wait to be approached instead of actively and bullishly seeking out opportunities. We wait for the one "big idea" or the "big opportunity" to come along, or we hide behind excuses like, "I'll do it when I have the money" or "I'll do it when I have more time." We say, "I'll do it when the kids start childcare/school/university/leave home."

We obsess over outcomes and "what ifs" at the expense of getting into action and trying something. We rely too much on external advice and depend on external forces to give us cues. I see it all the time when I give speeches. Afterward, people will come up to me and say, "So, what's your advice for me?" They wait for a genius answer, and a blueprint for their life to fall from my mouth. They always look quite shocked and a little ashen when I tell them, "I don't know what's right for you. Only you can know that."

If we just sit still and really listen to ourselves—listen to the call of the inner voice that knows what's up—we can hear it. Instead, we run around asking everyone, "What do you think I should do? What would you do if you were me?"

In the process of soul-searching with a bunch of souls that aren't ours, we lose valuable time that could have been spent looking inward and making a start. I've never fallen prey to this analysis paralysis because I don't allow myself to overthink. Does this idea feel right? Does it excite me? If the answer is yes, then I get going.

Say yes and figure out the rest later

Amazon's current market value is $916 billion, and its founder, Jeff Bezos, credits a lot of its growth to high-velocity decision-making. One of the ways Amazon is able to do this is by making decisions with only 70 percent of the key information available. Bezos says that if you wait for 90 percent or more, you're probably moving too slowly.

Some of the best decisions of my life have been the fastest ones I've made. My husband, Rowan, and I moved in together after dating for less than a month. We got engaged after six months, got married the next year, and three months later we were pregnant with our first child.

"A year from now you may wish
you had started today."

KAREN LAMB

I found the courage to start building a recruitment agency at the age of eighteen—an exercise for which I was completely unqualified. I had no experience and no knowledge, but I found the guts to do it and the grit to stick it out. I was twenty-four when I bought Business Chicks, and it didn't even cross my mind to be scared. I did all this by listening to what felt right in my head and heart, and not running around asking everyone if I should go for it.

When you know, you know. And when you don't know, you decide.

A few years ago, Business Chicks toured Seth Godin around Australia. Seth is a speaker, writer, and blogger, but those descriptions don't really do him justice. He's part marketing genius and part business guru, and of all the amazing people I've worked with, he speaks the most sense. I was pumped to be presenting him because I knew he'd make a massive impact on anyone who was lucky enough to hear him speak.

One of the people in our audience that day was a woman named Jen Bicknell. Jen was a partner at a law firm, and had been for almost nine years. She was a loyal Business Chicks devotee, so knowing she'd get value from the experience no matter what, she booked into the event without even knowing who Seth was.

Seth's words that day evoked something in Jen. He said that if you want anything big to happen in your life, you need to stop waiting for permission. "No one is going to pick you," he said. "You've got to pick yourself."

Jen ran back to the office after the event, not entirely knowing what to do with her excitement. She knew she'd witnessed something re-markable, and that something had just shifted within her. Jen spent the next six weeks completely immersed in every book Seth had written and said she came to the realization that although she was happy, she was just coasting and not challenging herself. Deep down, she realized that she really needed to run her own business, so that's what she set out to do.

In the weeks that followed, Jen decided to go it alone and quit the law firm. These days, she runs her own law consultancy firm, and continues to consult for her previous employer. When she said yes to trying something new, Jen didn't know exactly what that would look like. But if she hadn't had the guts to try, she'd probably still be left wondering.

One of my favorite stories of saying yes comes from television producer, screenwriter, and author Shonda Rhimes, who is the brains behind shows like *Scandal*, *Grey's Anatomy*, and *How to Get Away with Murder*. On Thanksgiving in 2013, Shonda was having dinner with her sister Delores and telling her about some of the invitations she was receiving as her profile continued to grow in the industry. Speaking engagements, Hollywood parties . . . you name the opportunity, and Shonda was being offered it. But her sister remained indifferent to Shonda's musings.

"Who cares?" Delores said. "You never say yes to anything, anyway."

It was in that moment, and hearing those comments from her sister, that forced Shonda to realize that despite her success, she was hiding from life and was miserable as a result. So in her sister's dining room that night Shonda vowed to say yes to unexpected invitations and opportunities.

For one year, she said yes to anything that made her nervous and anything that forced her out of her comfort zone—speaking in public, going on live television, meeting with the president of the United States, losing 100 pounds. In doing so, she changed her life. "The very act of doing the thing that scared me undid the fear and made it not scary," she said in a TED Talk, aptly named "My Year of Saying Yes to Everything."

Saying yes and figuring it out later might not mean starting a business, meeting with the president (go, Shonda!), or anything near as intimidating. Saying yes when you don't have all the answers might be as simple as going on a date with someone you're not convinced about or having that conversation for a new job even though you're happy where you are. Opportunities often arise from unexpected places—that serendipitous chat with someone in the office elevator, a chance meeting at the barbecue you weren't going to go to, or attending a business conference with a bunch of people you don't know. Starting by saying yes regularly to smaller situations may just be the door opener you need to reach bigger horizons.

What I love about Shonda's story of saying yes is that she didn't start with the intention of creating a TED Talk or writing a book. She said yes because she knew it was what she needed to do. When a publisher approached her about turning the year into a book, she said yes. After everything she had just created for herself, how could she not?

One foot in front of the other

One of the biggest lessons I've learned is that success is achieved through perpetual motion. It's about putting one foot in front of the other and keeping on walking, no matter what. You can have bad days and rest, and you can slow your walk down to a shuffle, but you just can't stop. The secret is to build the discipline (until it's second nature) to find a tiny way to move the game forward each day—an email here, a call there, even a session in the park, giving yourself the space to dream. That's all moving the game forward.

Former journalist and magazine editor Sarah Wilson is the first to admit her business started almost by accident. While researching a weekly newspaper column on how to make life better, she attempted to remove all sugar from her diet for two weeks. The success of that experiment led to the *I Quit Sugar* e-books. Fast-forward six years, and Sarah had built a business with twenty-three staff and a community of more than 2.3 million people through her website, eight-week program, and three bestselling books. Her message has been received far and wide, with her books and programs available in 113 countries and twelve languages.

Sarah could never have known where that one column would lead, and she couldn't have predicted the success that she created. For the most part, she was well and truly winging it. In fact, if she had sat down at the start and tried to imagine it all, there's a strong possibility she couldn't have. Instead, she went with the flow, maximizing opportunities, and as a result, her business became the success story it did.

In another beautiful example of winging it, without a firm plan of where she'll explore next, Sarah has now closed her business, trusting in her instincts that this is the right choice.

THE QUESTIONS THAT GUIDE ME

Sometimes questions are more
important than answers.

NANCY WILLARD

I've always believed that asking the right questions allows me to get to know others more deeply. We're often too busy talking and not asking enough intelligent questions, and as a result we miss out on the opportunity to truly connect.

One time I was having lunch with a girlfriend, Simone. Simone told me about the latest round of failed dates she'd had, and how exasperated she felt that she hadn't found a partner yet. Like many of us, her life hadn't eventuated into the expectation she had of it. She was on the other side of forty, and desperate (in her words) to have a child. She was open to having a baby on her own but was afraid and stuck as to which way to turn. Normally, we'd banter back and forth on this topic (it wasn't new territory in our friendship, as this was the most important thing in her world) and then move on to the next subject. This time, I wanted it to be different.

"Sim, we need to get real," I said. I paused, took a very deep breath, and asked her, "What are you really scared of?"

Simone burst into tears. She told me she was actually terrified of what other people would think if she were to have a baby on her own. She'd been raised in a very conservative family who had strong opinions on how a family should look, and she thought they'd be disappointed if she went it alone. Through tears, and a glass of champagne, we workshopped this together and by the end of the lunch she'd decided to set a plan in motion. Today, Simone is the solo parent to a gorgeous baby boy who is adored not only by Simone, but by Simone's family too.

In the same way that great questioning can open up a world of possibility for others, asking questions of ourselves from time to time can be incredibly helpful. Doing this promotes introspection, and ultimately helps us to decide what's important and what's not. Here are the questions I regularly ask myself, so I can always be lifting my game.

WHAT WOULD YOU DO IF YOU KNEW YOU COULD NOT FAIL? This question helps me remember that the only thing standing in the way of attempting something is the thought that I might fail at it. You too? We'd all try so much more if we weren't scared of falling on our faces. It could be applying for a job you've had your eye on, or asking someone out on a date, or even just starting back at the gym. An act of courage usually only takes a few seconds of "pain" and then it's over. The challenges that scare us are often like needles—we dread them so much, but they're never as bad as we imagine.

I use this question to *really* try to open my mind, not just to get through everyday tasks. This question gently nudges me to think larger and aim higher. When I was contemplating moving overseas (I'll get to that story soon) I pondered this question, and it helped me decide right then and there that the move was the right thing for us.

WHAT WOULD MAKE TODAY GREAT? Instead of writing a to-do list, I start each day with a fresh page in my notebook. At the top (instead of "to do") I just write, "What would make today great?" I try to imagine myself at the end of my day, having accomplished a few things and knowing that I've given my all, doing the important things that matter most. It can be as simple as writing a card to someone I haven't been in touch with for a while, or getting a major pitch in, or calling my mom, or booking a massage, or doing something that I know I've been putting off. It also helps me avoid falling into the busyness trap of trying to do too much.

The goal is to run your day, not have the day run you. By setting it up from the outset, and being clear about your intention, you're more likely to be inspired to achieve all that's on your list.

IF NOT NOW, THEN WHEN? This question sits on a sign above my desk, and it's a constant reminder that life is short and the "perfect" opportunity to start working toward a goal or dream you have may never arise. Too often we're stuck in "We'll get it done, one day" mode, when we all know that one day may never come.

Nigella Lawson, the British food personality, spoke for Business Chicks a while back, and I loved her take on this one. The emcee asked what Nigella's best piece of advice was and she said, "Do it now." When prompted to explain a little deeper, Nigella said she was a fan of getting things done as soon as you think of them. She said we waste so much time thinking about a task or a project, or even an email, and that her advice would be to just get that thing done straightaway.

So many of my tasks don't make it to my to-do list because I just get them done when I think of them. Or I do them immediately, then afterward I write them on the list so I can get the satisfaction of ticking them off. (I bet you've been guilty of this too.)

HAVE I DONE ANYTHING WORTH REMEMBERING LATELY? When it comes down to it, we're all the same. We have jobs and families, and we eat and sleep. It's what we do outside of these things that makes us interesting and gets us remembered. My friend Narelle was once on a business trip in rural China, which happened to coincide with her birthday. It took me loads of effort to track her down at her hotel and organize to have a chocolate cake (her favorite) delivered to her room. The language barrier with the hotel was strong, and it took some super-sleuthing on my end, but the surprise it gave her was worth the effort, and she still talks about it to this day.

HOW LONG ARE YOU GOING TO BE DEAD? We only get one shot. Might as well go for it.

YOU CAN'T CONTROL ANYTHING OUTSIDE OF YOU

"When I was twenty-three I got an interview with an agent in LA. I didn't have any money to pay for my flights. At the time, I was doing one segment a week on morning TV that paid $300 a pop—so I called my friend who ran a cleaning company and asked if I could clean toilets to pay for my flights!

I made it to LA., sat in front of the agents, and the best part of the story was they signed me on the spot, then dropped me as soon as I got back home. But I didn't care! That was an awesome lesson in winging it—failing and still believing in yourself!"

LOLA BERRY
nutritionist and author

GETTING YOUR HEAD RIGHT

I get asked all the time if entrepreneurs are born or made.

In my case, I think I was born one. I'm the eldest of three kids, and although it's not politically correct to describe young girls this way anymore, my mom would tell you I was bossy. I'm quick to tell her I was gearing up to be a leader.

My dad was an accountant, and my mom is a teacher. Even though I grew up wanting for nothing and was very safe, secure, and loved, I always had a sense that there was a bigger world out there to explore.

I was the kid tugging at my mom's skirt, incessantly asking questions and interrupting every conversation she tried to have. At the age of eight, I took the pocket money I'd been saving and without telling my parents caught the train to go and buy my first record (Rick Astley, of course) a couple of suburbs away. My mom was enraged and exasperated when I got home. "What if something had happened to you? What if you'd gotten lost?" I've always found it's easier to beg for forgiveness than ask for permission, and I knew they'd never in a million years have let me go if I'd asked. I've since spent pretty much my whole life doing the same: pushing the boundaries of what's considered acceptable and cleaning it up whenever things go wrong.

I was the one who'd round up all the other kids on the street and get them together in my backyard. I'd stand up on a milk crate to get their attention, telling them all to go and borrow some money from their parents and bring it back to the group. I'd then lead them up to the shops and buy as many packets of candy as we could carry. Back home we'd divvy up the haul into smaller packages, and we'd sell those smaller packages back to the parents. The trick was that we made money by selling the candy at a profit, but we also never repaid the original investment (because we were still cute and our parents were all so delighted by our genius initiative), so it was a double-profit kind of situation.

My next-door neighbor owned a restaurant up the road, and from the age of twelve, I started begging her for a job. She'd always remind

"If opportunity doesn't knock,
build a door."

MILTON BERLE

me that it was illegal to work before I turned fourteen, but I kept try-ing to convince her, saying, "No one will know!" When eventually I did reach the legal age, she relented and gave me a job on Friday and Saturday nights waiting tables, polishing cutlery, making the garlic bread, and schmoozing the customers. I accepted every shift offered to me and saved every dollar I could.

My immediate goal was to get myself a car, and I bought one when I was fifteen. It was my first lesson in doing something before I was ready, because at that age, I wasn't legally allowed to drive. That car went on to become the center of the universe for my friends and me. It was a beat-up, light-blue Daihatsu Charade that cost $1,500. I thought I was cooler than Rachel from *Friends*, decking it out with fluffy black-and-white animal-print seat covers and a tree-shaped air freshener that I proudly hung over the rearview mirror. One time, with the Backstreet Boys's "As Long As You Love Me" blaring through the speakers and a car full of girlfriends singing at the top of their lungs, I tried to get to the rooftop parking lot at the shops near our school. Halfway up the ramp, the car started rolling backward. I slammed my foot on the brake and yelled at everyone to get out. Even with all the girls out of the car, it wouldn't budge. In a damsel-in-distress moment (the first and probably last of my life), a bunch of pimple-faced teenage schoolboys came to push it up the ramp, saving the day. That was the last time I ever attempted big slopes in that little blue car.

Entrepreneurship is a mindset

I use the word "entrepreneur" a lot because it's what I most closely identify with. For me, that word encompasses a whole heap more than just a person who owns and runs a business.

Being an entrepreneur is about going first and taking risks. It's about playing big and thinking globally. It's about not being satisfied with where you are and always being curious about how you might improve.

Even though I showed some entrepreneurial qualities from a young age, I believe that entrepreneurship can live in anybody, and it's something that can be learned. I employ a ton of people who are entrepreneurial, even though they don't own their own businesses. They have that get-up-and-go attitude, they love trying new things, and they thrive on challenges. They're constantly questioning the status quo and don't have much regard for coloring within the lines or doing things the way they've always been done.

> Things move along so rapidly nowadays that people saying: "It can't be done," are always being interrupted by somebody doing it.
> **PUCK** MAGAZINE

Some of the most popular entrepreneurs of our time got to where they are because they refused to fit in or do things just like everyone else. These entrepreneurs help us to expand our thinking and encourage us to stop being so damn vanilla and safe all the time. Spanx's Sara Blakely once flashed her underwear in one of her first pitch meetings to illustrate a point. Tesla's Elon Musk paid for his college education by throwing parties and charging a five-dollar cover fee. And there are no stories more famous than that of Steve Jobs, who took Apple's slogan of "Think Different" to the extreme, reportedly not wearing shoes and washing his feet in the office restrooms. Now, few of us have the chutzpah to flash our knickers in meetings or the genius to envision a new phone that over a billion people will go on to buy, but we can work on the bit we can control: the big round mass that sits between our ears.

If you believe you can or can't, you're right

Steve Jobs was all kinds of eccentric, but underpinning his success was a belief that he could make a difference. In his mind, he simply believed he could.

No matter what your goal is or what you're trying to achieve, it all starts with getting your head right. Having the right mindset is one of the greatest predictors of success. It trumps intelligence, creativity, and appetite for risk. When you believe you can improve and grow, you have a growth mindset. If you're struggling with achieving your dreams, it may be because you believe that your abilities are static. If that's you, you've got what's called a fixed mindset.

A growth mindset is needed if you're ever to make it in business—be it your own or someone else's. To make it as an entrepreneur, you're going to have to cope with being knocked down over and over again. You have to learn to keep getting up. And you have to make your recovery faster each time. The good news is that recovering quickly from the everyday knockbacks and moving on as fast as possible is a skill that you can master. Over the years, I've trained myself to look for the silver lining in every situation, no matter how bad it may seem at first. Staying positive, keeping perspective about the size of your problem, and being grateful are useful tools when trying to cultivate a growth mindset.

Of course, just saying, "Be positive and think positive thoughts!" really helps no one, and we all need to walk a practical path in order to work on our mindsets. Here are a few things that have always worked for me when I've felt down or like I'm treading water and not getting anywhere.

KEEP A GRATITUDE JOURNAL IN THE MORNING. Starting your day by being intentionally thankful is the best form of therapy and is a sure-fire way to get you in the right frame of mind. When you give yourself just three minutes of space to write down what you already appreciate, the day ahead suddenly feels conquerable, no matter what's on your agenda. Get good at making gratitude easy for you too—don't hide that journal away in a drawer where you'll forget to dig it out. Keep it right by your bedside with your favorite pen on top, ready to go each day. If you can't manage the mornings, then try at night instead—whatever works for you!

MEDITATE AT NIGHT. I'd love to be a better sleeper, and I've really tried hard to work on my nighttime routines and rituals. It's near impossible with all the kids and how frequently they come in and out of our bedroom, but I have found that one helpful thing is to do a guided meditation before I sleep. It just brings me back to my breath, back to the now, and helps give me the best chance at setting things up for a good night's sleep. We all know that when we get quality sleep, being in the right mindset the next day is all the easier.

GET CLEAR ON WHAT'S IMPORTANT. It's easy to feel distracted, despondent, and defeated when you're shooting for other people's goals. When we're unsure of our own values and what we will and won't stand for, we can all get led in the wrong direction. Coming back to a simple evaluation of what you want and jotting down what's really important to you is a great way to land back in the right mindset. Often we're set off kilter because we're looking sideways too much, at what others are attempting to do. I've always found tremendous comfort in thinking "What is meant to be mine will be mine" and I've committed that mantra to heart, often repeating it when I'm disappointed about an outcome. Something shifts when you lift your thinking to being a little more patient and philosophical about the timing of your life, and it all becomes a lot lighter.

STOP SEEKING APPROVAL FROM OTHERS. Adopting a growth mindset is entirely an internal game. It's the stories you tell yourself and the strategies you employ that help you believe whatever you're working toward is achievable. Start playing the game by switching off the opinions and expectations of others. Tune back in to what you want, knowing that you're worthy enough to go for it. A minute spent seeking validation from other people is a minute wasted. You'll know you're on the right path when it appears, so look inward and get on your way!

Be pragmatic, not dramatic

Someone once said to me, "Emma, if you were any calmer, you'd be dead," which I immediately took as a compliment. Calmness can be a superpower, but here's the thing: I reckon anyone can master it. Over the years, I've practiced reacting calmly to any and all situations, and now being calm is just second nature to me.

It was a big deal for us to sign our very first major sponsor with one of Australia's largest banks in the early days of Business Chicks. I can hand-on-heart say that I gave that partnership my all. I referred countless clients to them, flew to their headquarters almost weekly for progress meetings, and bent over backward whenever they needed it. I was so grateful for their support, but I also knew we were giving them a ton of value for the investment they were making.

After three years, there was a changing of the guard at the bank, with a new manager stepping in to run the partnership. Like many new relationships, this one was a little rocky at first. The new manager didn't really understand Business Chicks yet, nor did he understand the value we brought or the work we'd previously executed. Nevertheless, he assured us that the partnership would carry on just as it always had, which was encouraging, as the contract was coming to an end in a few months' time.

We threw ourselves into that new relationship, and it really felt as though we were progressing by leaps and bounds. The new manager kept assuring us that women were important to the bank and that the sponsorship was a long-term play for them. Before we knew it, the day had come for the new contract to be executed. I was all set to fly in to their city to sign the documents, but on the Thursday night before our meeting, the manager texted me to say they weren't re-signing.

In the few minutes that followed, I swore a lot. Cushions were thrown. Wine was poured. However, once the initial shock had worn off and my rage had subsided, I sprang into action, canceling my flights and masterminding our next move. That same night, we got in touch with a different bank, one that was desperate to work with us, and scheduled lunch with them the next day. By 4:00 p.m. on the following Monday, we were sitting on the nineteenth floor of their office tower, signing a bigger and more meaningful contract than the previous partnership. As it turned out, women were important to this bank too.

Life throws curveballs at us all the time. A valued staff member will leave. An accounting error will cost a bucketload. You'll lose a client, or a competitor will copy your idea. You'll be laid off. An illness will come out of nowhere.

We have a saying around our office that is so embedded in our culture that it's even written into all our job descriptions. We call it "pragmatic, not dramatic." It basically means that when faced with a challenge (or a mini-panic), you should take a deep breath, do your best to exercise ease and grace, and get into solution-making mode as quickly as you can, rather than catastrophizing.

Here are some examples for you.

A DRAMATIC PERSON thinks the worst and immediately jumps to all the things that could further go wrong.

A PRAGMATIC PERSON gets into action and finds solutions with an even temperament and positive outlook.

A DRAMATIC PERSON talks behind people's backs and stimulates rumors. They love to talk for the sake of having their voice heard and probably have a "woe is me" mentality.

A PRAGMATIC PERSON has honest conversations with their peers and colleagues and asks for help when it's needed.

A DRAMATIC PERSON apportions blame to others and gets stuck in victimhood.

A PRAGMATIC PERSON will take accountability for whatever part they had to play in the situation, but won't dwell on it. They'll focus on solutions instead of pointing the finger at others.

A DRAMATIC PERSON overthinks any feedback they receive.

A PRAGMATIC PERSON listens to others' feedback and takes it on board with a levelheaded approach, always trying to see the world from another person's viewpoint.

Faced with being either of these people in a moment of pressure, I know which one I'd rather be. How about you?

Shit happens, and it happens to all of us. At the risk of sounding like a Hallmark card, every problem has a solution, and most problems present huge opportunities even though they totally suck at the time. The trick is to take the emotion out of your challenges and not seek unnecessary attention or sympathy.

Recovering from failure is all about fighting the instinct to retreat back into your comfort zone. I could have very easily become a victim and played the blame game that night, but whenever I get knocked down, I always use that failure to fuel my next move. Yep, I may swear on occasion, drink a glass of wine (or vodka, if the situation calls for it), and throw stuff around the house, but you'll never see me open a pack of Reese's and collapse on the sofa in defeat. I'm all about getting my head right as quickly as possible and then dreaming up ways to achieve a goal that is even more ambitious than the one I just failed at.

As leaders (and we all have the opportunity to be leaders, no matter what our role or status), our people look to us to set the tone. They look to us for guidance on how they should respond and act. While we might not always remember it, our people are always looking to us and, perhaps subconsciously, evaluating and learning from the way we conduct ourselves. A pragmatic, fair, and positive leader will always trump a leader who wants to create drama where there's really no space for it in the workplace.

You'll see your culture shift when you lead the way on being pragmatic and not dramatic. Removing the drama helps you focus on solutions and puts you back in control.

DO THE THING THAT SCARES YOU

If I think about the times when I've taken too long to make decisions on things I really wanted to do, the main reason was fear. Fear of not having enough money. Fear that I wasn't good enough. Fear that I'd fail. When I finally pushed through the fear and committed to the choice I knew deep down I wanted to make, none of those things proved true.

When I was living in Australia, a wonderful author named Kathy Lette recommended me to the producers on a television show called *Today*. They did their research, called me for a chat, and offered me a spot on a morning segment, talking about the news. I'm a huge advocate of the "say yes immediately and figure it out later" school of thought, but I falter at times too. I told them I'd check my calendar and get back to them, which was code for, "Ah, I don't think I'm good enough, but give me a moment to convince myself that I am and then I'll call you back."

I gave it an hour, called them back, and accepted their offer. Two days later I found myself in the makeup chair at the studios questioning why I'd signed up for this. Butterflies were racing around my stomach; I had absolutely no idea what I was doing. But I wasn't about to let on.

The producer came in to welcome me, offered me a coffee, and then handed me a sheet of paper with three topics to talk about. She gave me a friendly smile, told me the green room was "that way" for when I was finished in makeup, wished me luck, and disappeared.

"That's it?" I thought, but no one else seemed particularly worried, so I decided maybe I shouldn't be worried either. After I'd finished in makeup, I navigated the studio's corridors and located what I thought was the green room, momentarily wondering if anyone would find me there. Eventually someone did come to collect me and handed me over to a technician who fitted my microphone. Moments later that technician pointed over to the couch on set and whispered, "Okay, you, go."

I took my seat next to the hosts, heard a commanding voice from the dark say, "All quiet on set, please," followed immediately by a "three-two-one" countdown, which made me think, "Okay, I think this is the part where they want us to start talking." So that's precisely what I did.

There's nothing like a bit of live morning television action to get the heart racing, especially when you have no idea what you're doing. It makes you think on your feet and wing it like a pro, just like I did that first day.

Of course, once I figured out the system and the pace at which it all moved, I came to love every minute of my time on the show. I always think about this experience when I'm faced with a challenge I assume I might not be able to conquer. If someone else deems you capable, then you probably are. You've just got to fake it 'til you make it and believe it for yourself.

Growing up, we had a family tradition on birthdays. Just after we'd blown out the candles on our cake, Mom would delightfully recount in great detail the birth story of whoever's birthday it happened to be. All I remember hearing about was stitches and blood and seventeen hours of pain and the fact that my mom couldn't walk for a week afterward.

While it was all in jest, and probably pretty funny at the time, these stories subliminally terrified me, and somewhere along the line I convinced myself that I would never have children. I was certain there was no way I could go through what my mom had been through.

Eventually, I met Rowan and we got married and a few months later I peed on a stick and two lines appeared. As my belly started to grow, I became acutely aware that the baby was going to have to come out somehow. And so, with fierce resolution, I threw myself into watching every birth video I could, reading tons of birthing books, and enrolling in a few different prenatal classes too.

At that stage, my husband had an even more ignorant view of birth than me. He thought the way to have a baby was to check into a hospital and . . . well, he didn't know much more than that. He showed zero interest in the upcoming birth and thought he was hilarious, joking to everybody, "I don't care what happens, just as long as I'm north of the blue sheet and can't see anything."

After a few months of intense research, I felt a lot more educated and empowered. I was still scared of the possibilities for my birth experience, but remained unwavering about finding one that would suit me. I'd worked myself into a position of having lots of knowledge, but at some point, I needed to let go of it all and do what felt right to me.

I started to think that maybe I could have a natural birth and, being a person who takes everything to the extreme and likes to win (even when I'm just competing against myself), I challenged myself to the most natural experience I could possibly have: a planned home birth. Given that I was strong and healthy and my pregnancy was considered low-risk, this option really appealed to me.

My first daughter, Milla, was born by candlelight one early morning in May. There wasn't a blue sheet in sight, and my husband, midwife, and doula were all by my side. We set up a birthing pool in our bedroom, and Milla was born into the water, with her eyes wide open. She didn't cry once as I lifted her up out of the water. She just looked me straight in the eyes. It was the most liberating and fear-free experience I've ever had. That experience ignited a love of birth in me, and also showed me that other people's fears need not be my own. Sorry, Mom.

I've gone on to have five more planned home births, each one better than the last. All of the kids were around to experience our sixth baby's birth, which I loved.

While I appreciate that birth is a deeply personal experience for everyone, the strategy I took for getting what I wanted is the same one I've used in business and life: I worked hard on my mindset, put in the work, surrounded myself with competent people, and eventually convinced myself I could do it.

As Sheryl Sandberg points out in *Lean In,* "Fear is at the root of so many of the barriers that women face. Fear of not being liked. Fear of making the wrong choice. Fear of drawing negative attention. Fear of overreaching. Fear of being judged. Fear of failure. And the holy trinity of fear: the fear of being a bad mother/wife/daughter."

> # Doubt kills more dreams than failure ever will.
> ## SUZY KASSEM

I've seen this play out countless times with the women I meet, who confide their fears in me.

Sarah Pearce is the founder of Travelshoot, a business I love. Travelshoot connects travelers with photographers around the world, creating awesome pictures in front of the Eiffel Tower, for example, or on the Brooklyn Bridge, or even on the banks of a river in Queenstown.

Sarah has been a Business Chicks member for years, so I was happy when she sought my advice for raising her first round of capital. Raising money for your start-up is challenging at the best of times, but Sarah was also pregnant. She was worried about what potential investors would say and think. I asked Sarah if being pregnant had changed anything, and of course it hadn't. She was still as committed and passionate about seeing her business succeed, and even more resolute to raise the money to get it there. I told her to stand her ground, be proud, and that her being pregnant would sort out the types of investors she could work with really quickly. Those who were concerned were not the types she'd want to partner with anyway. Sarah went on to secure $700,000 in seed funding, and also negotiated three months of maternity leave into her agreement. Sarah's business continues to flourish while she's raising her sweet little family, proving that her fears were worth conquering.

I'm not for a second doubting that fear can be the most debilitating emotion. I've been racked with fear many times, particularly early in my career when I had to pick up the phone to call someone I didn't know or walk into a room full of strangers. I decided early on that I'd have to work on this, and today I have a very healthy relationship with fear.

Over the years, I've learned that you simply must do the things that scare you. Just say yes, even when there's a part of you that wants to say no. Once you're committed, you're not allowed to look back or change your mind until it's done. I was scared to quit college, but I did it. I was scared to move to America, which is *why* I did it. I was scared to give

"Dream big. Start small.
But most of all, start."

SIMON SINEK

birth, which is why I did it six times (and at home!), and I was scared to hire a CEO and hand the reins of my company over. Facing my fears on all of these things only built my confidence and made me more courageous, which is precisely why I attempted them all.

Of course, you can practice being fearless without the need to give birth, move countries, or hire senior leaders. It's often in the small actions that we find our courage. On the final night of our most recent conference, I led a conga line around the dance floor and outside to the pool area. I jumped into the pool fully clothed, and a number of our members jumped in right behind me.

One member, Kristine, hesitated. "I can't!" she said. I challenged her with, "Why not?" "I've got my clothes on!" she said. Bobbing up and down in the pool in my gold pumps and still completely dressed, I laughed and shouted, "So do I! Just jump in!" After a little more coercing, Kristine took a deep breath and jumped into the pool with the rest of us. And what was the outcome? The applause of about twenty other women and one very happy Kristine. Facing fear feels great.

What I know now is that if I'm not putting myself in an uncomfortable situation, I'm not content. I'm happiest when there's something in my future that makes me a little uncomfortable. It energizes me, in the same way it energized Sarah and Kristine, to think that I'm going to do something that I've never done before. It may be giving a speech to the biggest crowd I've ever faced, or it may be some sort of physical challenge—anything that makes me stretch into a form a little bit greater than who I am today.

Here are some of the most common excuses I hear from people who are letting fear get in the way of the things they really want to do and why I think they are excuses that can be conquered:

"I DON'T HAVE THE SKILLS." First, let's define skills a little more. Are you talking about the hard skills required to get some jobs technically done, or the soft skills required to get ahead? Whatever is getting in the way can be learned. We're lucky these days to have access to so much knowledge and information that doesn't necessarily require us to have worked in a role for a long period of time. You want to learn how to code? Write a screenplay? Touch-type? Drive a truck? These are all skills that we can access relatively quickly if we have the right level of determination and the ability to focus. The accumulation of soft skills—resiliency, adaptability, social skills, problem-solving, leadership abilities, etc.—these are all within your reach and should be seen as an ongoing collection as your career grows. You don't merely learn them and then stop. It's a lifelong curation of mistakes and growth, mistakes and growth.

A long-held misconception is that hard skills are more important than soft skills, but with the advent of artificial intelligence taking over many of the more technical roles, there's never been a better time to focus on developing your soft skills. In fact, the *Wall Street Journal* surveyed 900 CEOs and found that 92 percent reported soft skills as being just as important as technical skills. You *can* learn the skills, so start learning them.

"I DON'T KNOW WHERE TO START." That's a cop-out. While precious few of us ever know the exact path we have to take to reach our goals, we can all think of one small action we can take now to get going. Just one. Make a phone call. Book a coffee with someone. Research something. Write down your idea or vision. Open a bank account. Buy a new pen and notepad. Anything—just start!

"I'M SCARED OF WHAT PEOPLE WILL THINK." It's completely natural to want to be liked, accepted, and thought highly of. That's human nature and it plagues us all. It's also completely natural to strive to be the best version of yourself you can be, and if you're paralyzed thinking about what others think of you, then you're not striving for that version of yourself. Living your life according to the rules and expectations of others who you feel are judging you at any given moment is a fast way to not truly live. Perhaps it's time to take a hard look at the people in your life and decide whether they're really supporting your growth.

Surrounding yourself with positive people who believe in you and will back your dreams no matter what will surely lessen the amount of time you spend worrying about what others think. If this is truly a problem for you, then go talk with someone about it. Getting clear on your motivations and self-limiting beliefs with a therapist or someone else you trust might help shift this one out of your way.

> I would rather choke on greatness than nibble on mediocrity.
>
> **UKNOWN**

"I MIGHT FAIL." At some stage, you probably will. On the flip side, you'll learn a bunch of stuff about yourself along the way. Something enlightening happens when you persevere, though, and every so often the perseverance gods smile down and reward you with a convincing win for all that effort you invested. In 1978, marathon swimmer Diana Nyad was twenty-eight years old when she first attempted to swim from Cuba to Key West, Florida. She swam for forty-two hours before doctors removed her from the water, fearing her safety in rough seas. After giving up swimming soon after, and working for almost thirty years as a sports journalist, in 2011, Diana decided to try again, this time without a shark cage. She was sixty-one years old at the time. She failed twice that year, once after she suffered an asthma attack and once more after suffering life-threatening jellyfish stings. In August 2012, a lightning storm ruined her fourth attempt. But on her fifth attempt, at the age of sixty-four years old, those perseverance gods were looking down in awe, cheering her on. In 2013, thirty-five years after her first attempt, Diana became the first person to ever swim from Cuba to Florida without the assistance of a shark cage. Imagine if Diana had been stuck in the "I might fail" excuse. She'd forever be left wondering "what if?" and we'd all be robbed of this incredible tale of simply refusing to give up hope.

"I DON'T HAVE THE MONEY." Yeah, that old chestnut. Very few of us, the trust-fund babies excluded, start out with a limitless checkbook. The good news is that money is relatively easy to come by these days. It might take some uncomfortable conversations and it might take a lot of rejections but there *are* people out there looking to diversify their well-earned dollars into something that's not just the stock market or property. Well-seasoned entrepreneurs often get to a point where they like to be reminded of their younger selves and are excited to come across people who have the same ambition and drive and ideas as they once had when they started out (hint: that's you!). If you're not looking for an investor, then could you partner up with someone else who can share your start-up costs? Could you save a little more each week in order to build a small pool from which to start? Creativity is always needed when it comes to starting out in business, but it's not an insurmountable problem or an excuse we should hide behind.

I see it as my responsibility, as the leader of a movement like Business Chicks, to hold a space for others to explore their relationship with fear and to wing it a little more each day. I'd hate to think you didn't achieve your dreams on account of fear, because it's a reason that's not good enough.

PLAY A BIGGER GAME

Great minds discuss ideas; average minds discuss events; small minds discuss people.
UNKNOWN

At Business Chicks, we talk a lot about playing a bigger game— encouraging our members to open their eyes and lift their thinking. Playing a bigger game means something different for everyone. It's not as simple as having a bigger company or earning a bigger paycheck. It's much more than that. For some, playing a bigger game may mean finding the courage to do something for the first time or speaking up where you've stayed silent before.

For me, playing a bigger game means challenging my ways of thinking, reimagining long-held beliefs, and being open to new possibilities.

Playing a bigger game also means not focusing on the minutiae of my life and my problems. Those things just don't get my energy. It's about lifting my thinking and focusing on how I can make a contribution to the wider world without just living inside of mine.

When we think big, there's no room for small thinking. Suddenly, the trivia of who said what and who's doing what fades into the background. The small issues that can consume your energy have no place inside your big vision.

I'm lucky to have a number of wonderful mentors, and Sir Richard Branson sits at the top of that list. Each time we meet, I'm reminded to think bigger and live a little larger. A few years ago, we were talking about doing business in Australia (where I'd had my company for ten years) and he interjected with, "Is it even possible to make money in Australia?" His big-picture thinking made me stop. I decided that I needed to step it up.

At the time of that conversation with Richard, all was going well. We were making good profits each year; we had a beautiful team and a great culture. I was financially stable, personally and in the business. However, when I really sat with the harsh truth of my life, it was clear that, even with the busyness of kids and a reasonably sized business, I was cruising. I can't stand feeling like I'm not growing and knew something big had to shift.

After talking with Richard, I decided to launch Business Chicks into the US.

I was heavily pregnant with our fourth child at the time, but I threw myself into the challenge as if I were sleeping ten hours a night and this was my first baby.

I'd get up before our household woke each morning and be sitting at the local café before the coffee machines had warmed up so I could catch the tail end of the workday in New York. After I'd worked in peace for a bit, I'd race home, get the kids ready for the day, get myself ready (always in that order, of course), and then head in to the office.

My Australian team was exceptional, staying through the night on many occasions so we could catch the US in their time zone, enticed only by red wine, pizza, and lots of laughs about the people on the other side of the world who couldn't understand our accents. I've never seen a team so passionately devoted to making a dream happen. It'd be 1:00 a.m. Sydney time, and we'd be working in the boardroom together and one of my team would yell out, "I just heard back from a company and they're going to buy two tables at our New York event—we're doing this, Em!"

Our series of launch events was spectacular. We packed ballrooms in Los Angeles, New York City, and San Francisco. It was thrilling to watch American women marvel at the experience for the first time—the scale and joy of it all—just as I had many years before.

Rowan wasn't with me for the launches, but when I got home, he said, "That looked really amazing. Would you ever consider moving there?"

The idea of that felt really big and scary. So I said, "Absolutely, let's do it."

Six months later, my family and I packed up our lives and moved from Australia to the US, closing the loop on that conversation I'd had with Richard less than a year before. There were a number of times in the six months between deciding to move and getting on the plane that I wanted to take back my "Yes." It all seemed too hard. Our family would miss us. There was a big financial risk. I wondered if the kids would get a better education in Australia. I seriously asked myself if I could create more impact by playing it safe and staying. But in the spirit of playing a bigger game, I knew in my heart what had to be done.

Would we have moved if we'd known how hard it was going to be? Probably not. The magic always lies in the not knowing. But more on that later. In the meantime, here are a few signs you might be playing it too safe and it might be time to start playing a bigger game.

YOU'RE A BIT BORED. We've all been there. Boredom is a great indicator that we could be striving for more. There's a difference between being content and being bored. The good news is that boredom has an easy remedy: you just do more! Think about a creative project you've been wanting to start for ages, or a new goal you might want to tackle. Go volunteer somewhere that'll have a big impact or seek out new people to learn from. You're lacking growth and stimulation, so it's time to go hunt them down.

YOU WAIT TO BE ASKED. Nothing strips possibility from a situation as fast as sitting back and waiting to see what happens, hoping that someone might just notice your needs. Practice asking for what you want and need, over and over, until it no longer feels uncomfortable. Also get comfortable with being told no from time to time—that's all part of the process. What matters is that you didn't sit back, wait to be asked, and then sit in resentment that no one noticed you.

YOU'RE HITTING YOUR GOALS TOO EASILY. Lucky you. Now go set some bigger ones. You're a clever soul capable of a lot more.

YOU'RE ENVIOUS OF OTHER PEOPLE. Time to take a long, hard look in the mirror. What is it that you see lacking in yourself that is making you envious of others? Are you envious of their relationship? Their new job? Their financial situation? All of these signs are just life's way of wanting you to wake up and take action in these areas. Let's take the focus and attention off of others, turn it back on ourselves, and start to make the changes we really want.

THERE'S AN IDEA THAT YOU JUST CAN'T STOP THINKING ABOUT. That's your intuition's way of trying to tell you to listen up and go make that dream happen. Don't give a moment's thought to whether it's possible or not, if you're going to fail at it or not—just go and try to make it happen.

YOU'RE SPENDING TOO MUCH TIME ON SOCIAL MEDIA. Avoidance of life right there! If you find yourself mindlessly trawling through social media, stop yourself and be tough enough to put up some boundaries. Start by giving yourself a small goal—"I will not go on social media for the next hour"—and work your way up to having one day a week away from all channels. I do this regularly, and it makes such a difference to my well-being and happiness.

Who are you not to be?

In her book *A Return to Love*, one of my favorite thought leaders, Marianne Williamson, wrote, "Our deepest fear is not that we are inadequate; our deepest fear is that we are powerful beyond measure. It is our light, not our darkness that most frightens us. We ask ourselves, who am I to be brilliant, gorgeous, talented, and fabulous? Actually, who are you not to be?"

I love these words so much that I had them made into a huge decal for a wall in my office. It is a constant reminder for us all to step into our power, and not walk away from it.

Years ago, we toured with Professor Fiona Wood and presented her across Australia. Reading through Fiona's bio will make anyone feel like a massive underachiever: she is a mother of six and grandmother of three, is the director of the Burns Service of Western Australia, is the founder and a board member of the Fiona Wood Foundation, was named Australian of the Year in 2005, and as if that's not enough, she also invented the technology of spray-on skin.

She is without a doubt one of the most hardworking and impressive people I've ever met. Whenever I traveled with her, she'd sit in her seat on the plane and boot up her laptop straightaway. One time, she took the red-eye flight from Perth to Melbourne at 6:00 a.m. to speak for us at our 8:00 a.m. event. I think she'd managed three hours of sleep, but she was still full of energy, the type of person you'd want both in an emergency and at your Friday night dinner party.

There are so many things I love about the woman. Every time I hear her speak, I learn something new. Fiona, as well as addressing corporate audiences, gives a lot of her talks in schools. Every time she gives a speech at a school, she asks the students three questions: "How many times have you done something that's less than your best just so you can make others around you feel comfortable?" Apparently, all the kids in the room nod and say, "Yep, I do that all the time."

She then asks them, "How often are you energy in the raw? How often do you lift others up and take them with you?" All the kids sit there and shake their heads saying no, they'd never done that.

This isn't just reserved for kids either. Somewhere along the line, we learn to water ourselves down so that our achievements don't make others feel uncomfortable. We're often embarrassed by what we've accomplished, regularly accrediting our success to luck, or giving the credit to others who have helped along the way rather than taking it for ourselves. It's something I struggle with too, but I'm working on it, because who am I not to?

WORRY ABOUT YOURSELF

The compare and despair crisis

Too many people waste time worrying about what others are up to and stressing about what they'll do next. There's a temptation to obsess over other people's social media accounts, studying the lives that appear easier and more glamorous than ours, wondering if we're doing it right.

The most successful people I know are the ones who don't care what anyone else is up to. They simply don't have the time! They are so compelled by their own vision and their own dreams that wavering from them would only slow them down.

Eons ago, I used to do competitive aerobics (yep, that sport where you jump in the air and land in the splits, then spin around and do ten one-arm push-ups, all the while with a big smile on your face and a leotard going up your bum). My coach had a huge impact on me. He used to say, "Don't waste time comparing yourself to others. There will always be people who are better than you and people who will be worse. The only thing you need to worry about is 'Am I getting better?'"

That sounds easy to do, but when we're constantly interrupted by messages that capitalize on our insecurities, it becomes harder. Social media creates the illusion that everything we see on Instagram is reality. This does us no favors. It's tempting to believe that everyone is leading happier, more fulfilled lives than we are.

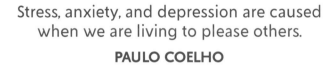

Stress, anxiety, and depression are caused when we are living to please others.
PAULO COELHO

Samantha Wills is an Australian accessory designer whose jewelry has been worn by countless celebrities and featured in magazines across the globe. Samantha is often referred to as an overnight success, but, like most entrepreneurs, she is a woman who has worked her backside off for more than a decade to grow her brand into what it is today.

In late 2017, after returning to her home in New York from a holiday in Mexico, Samantha wrote a post on her website about the Instagram photos she'd posted during her trip.

"Those photos tell a story of the happiest girl in the world!" she wrote. "I mean, look at her dancing on a beach! Laughing over a glass of pinot! World's biggest smile on her face, as she sits on a beach in her bathing suit, sipping a cocktail from a coconut."

But the reality, she wrote, was far from the images that were popping up on her account. She admitted she was "a shell of herself," medicated on Valium, fighting jet lag, drinking too much tequila, and having to continually apologize to friends for the streams of "hot, silent tears that would run down her face."

In what was one of the most powerful and vulnerable articles I've read, Samantha apologized to her (then) more than 220,000 followers for misleading them about what was really going on in her world. She apologized for her contribution to the ongoing problem of self-comparison on social media, and she vowed to make a commitment to being part of the solution.

I really hope Samantha's story will inspire women to go easy on themselves and stop believing the lies that social media perpetuates. We've all been guilty of posting beautiful photos and will continue to do so. That's not the crime. The crime is buying into the idea that everyone has it easier than we do because they're more beautiful, or make more money, or have more kids.

No one has it all sorted. We're all winging it as much as the next person.

Nothing is ever as it seems

My husband once went away for the night, and in a moment of optimism and boldness, I turned to the five kids we had at the time and suggested we head out to dinner. I packed them up and off we went. The kids pretty much exist on a diet of spaghetti and pizza (cool your jets—I sneak vegetables into the bolognese and have gotten them addicted to cauliflower pizza too, which they think is the real deal), so when I remembered a local Italian restaurant an Uber driver had recommended, the kids roared in agreement, and we were on our way.

The Isaacs clan is quite a sight en masse, I'm well aware. I always chuckle at the reactions we get whenever we enter a room together. At a recent Thanksgiving dinner, we were even asked to bring our own table and chairs because our host had no other way to accommodate us all.

This evening, as we sat down at our table at the restaurant, I smugly thought to myself, "I'm the real deal. Look at me! Here I am taking five kids out to dinner! I'm Mother of the Year!" I handed my phone to the waitress and asked her to take a photo that we could send to my hubby, who surely would be missing us all by now. (Who am I kidding? He was

"The woman who does not require validation
from someone is the most feared
individual on the planet."

MOHADESA NAJUMI

tucked up in some cool hotel room with the bed to himself, room service on speed dial, and Netflix cranking.)

And that's when it all turned to shit. My then six-year-old (Honey), who was high on the candy she'd nicked while we were waiting for our table, intercepted the phone, demanding to watch YouTube and starting the mother of all meltdowns when I said, "No way." The three-year-old (Ryder) swiped Indie's water (she's five), proceeding to spill it all over himself. Indie retaliated by pulling Ryder's hair so hard that she was left with a tuft of blond curls in her hand. Ryder then let loose the shrillest scream I have ever heard and scratched Indie across the face, drawing blood. Through her you-can't-have-YouTube tears, Honey shrieked, "There's blood!" so loudly that the entire restaurant went quiet for a split second, just as Indie struck back, punching Ryder so hard he fell sideways and let out another scream. I yelled at Indie, so now there were three of them crying, with me wishing I could too.

The nine-year-old (Milla) just rolled her eyes, the baby looked stunned, and for the next twenty minutes, the woman at the table closest to us was shaking her head at me in disbelief that I'd attempted to take five kids out for dinner—or even had them in the first place.

The truth is, most outings with five kids (well, mine anyway) on a Sunday night when they're tired and doing something out of their routine will end like this. But I'll admit that if I had somehow managed to sneak in a quick pic before it all fell apart, I would have definitely posted it, and anyone who saw it would still think of me as Mother of the Year, which is so far from the case.

The moral to the story? Be kinder to yourself, because nothing is ever as it seems on social media. Oh, and never trust an Uber driver for restaurant recommendations.

Make more moves and fewer announcements

Tania Austin is a brilliant but fiercely private businesswoman. I know she'll hate that I'm drawing attention to her, because she spends her time avoiding the spotlight and she's much more comfortable with highlighting the achievements of her team or her family. Tania, however, epitomizes the idea of making more moves and fewer announcements, and her story deserves to be told.

Tania's business, DECJUBA, has become a force to be reckoned with on the Australian fashion scene, with almost 130 stores across Australia and New Zealand. Tania quietly and humbly goes about achieving extraordinary growth, while at the same time being an exceptionally present and committed mother to her three children, and a passionate and generous philanthropist too. She does all of this with an unrivaled amount of humility and grace.

Don't for a minute confuse Tania's humility with a lack of ambition, though. She's one of the most ambitious people I've ever met, but she goes about life with an ease and elegance that we could all learn a thing or two from.

Every time I speak with Tania, she's up to something. There'll be a new property project going on, five new store openings in the works, she's hosting a girlfriend's birthday party, launching a new brand, taking her team to India on a leadership trip, or vacationing with her kids. You'd never know it, though, because Tania doesn't announce it all. She's moving at a rapid pace, making moves everywhere she goes, but she doesn't feel the need to tell the world.

When you're sure of yourself, you don't need to.

VIBES DON'T LIE

Many years ago now, I started to get to know a woman who'd run big businesses all around the world and, from what I could tell, was very well respected. We shared a couple of coffees and these progressed to lunches (generally at expensive restaurants—she paid, no matter how much I protested). I never really knew what she wanted with me—friendship, perhaps, but we didn't speak much at all about our personal lives, with business dominating all our conversations.

We'd known each other for under a year when she approached me with a business proposition. She wanted to partner with me to produce a huge event, flying in lots of international speakers, booking out mammoth venues, and acquiring big-ticket sponsorships. She made lots of promises of lucrative returns, but like a lot of pitches, it sounded a little too good to be true. I hesitated to jump in but couldn't quite put my finger on why.

There wasn't a lot on the outside to make me suspicious. This woman talked a very big game, had offices in many major cities around the world, name-dropped at every turn, lived in a nice house she told me she'd bought several years back, and always looked like she'd just stepped out of a salon.

Still, something just didn't feel right.

Dr. Libby Weaver is a nutritional biochemist, author, speaker, and one of my all-time favorite humans. She espouses the brilliant, helpful philosophy of "If it's not a hell yes, then it's a no." She says that if you don't get that immediate and overwhelming desire to say yes to a decision placed in front of you, then your answer probably needs to be no.

I didn't know Libby back then, but I wish I had as it would have made my decision to decline this woman's offer a lot easier. The business idea ended up being a flop. There was a lot of hot air around it in the media (this woman excelled at public relations), but ultimately only a handful of tickets sold and the event was canceled.

For someone who claimed to be so connected, it seemed odd that she couldn't pull it off. Next, by complete accident, I worked out that a dear friend of mine worked on the same floor of the building this woman had said her office was in, but her company wasn't there. Hmm. The final nail in the coffin was when another friend of mine who worked in real estate looked up this woman's house and found it was owned by someone else. You'd be forgiven for thinking I'm a stalker right about now, but I needed to know if my hunch was correct.

Looking back, I did know something was fishy. None of it felt right, but I let myself get bamboozled by her corporate jargon, her well-heeled appearance, and the circles she assured me she moved in. Even though it took me a while to catch on, I'm glad I did eventually trust my instincts.

One of the values I live by is "if it doesn't feel right, it isn't right." I use this when I don't know which way to turn, and it rarely lets me down.

As in any business, our leadership team grapples with people problems every day. No matter how strong your culture is, or how big your company becomes, managing and leading people will always throw up challenges. Every now and then, I'll have to have a conversation with my leaders about a team member who isn't working out or might just be a wrong cultural fit. I'll listen carefully as my leaders try and rationalize the situation to find a well-meaning solution like moving them around the business or changing their role to accommodate them.

Now I'm not for one moment proposing that we are unkind and move people out of our companies at the first available chance when something doesn't go our way. Of course we need solid human resources practices and we need to put people front and center of everything we do. However, coming back to the philosophy of "if it doesn't feel right, it isn't right" can be really useful in these sorts of conversations. We can move people around our companies as much as we like, but if someone is not right for our business and is upsetting our culture, then no amount of shuffling will fix the problem. I'll often be the one in the conversation to say, "I can see what we're trying to do here, but it doesn't matter what job we move this person to—they still won't be right."

Tuning in to what feels right (our intuition or gut instinct) can be harder for some. It's available to all of us, though, when we listen to the signs in our body and practice the following techniques.

SLOW DOWN. A surefire way to access more of our intuition is to slow down and allow space for some proper thinking time. Too often in our daily roles at the office we jump from decision to decision too quickly, only staying in the rational headspace and not accessing something deeper. If you can give yourself a few moments of peace and quiet to think about what your instincts are telling you, you'll often find a truth surfacing that might not have come up without giving it the time it deserved.

CALL ON PAST EXPERIENCES. Try to remember a time when you had a hunch about something and it was proven right. The more you can learn to trust yourself and your gut instincts, the more you'll be able to access them again for future decisions.

STOP OVERTHINKING. Overthinking robs us of so much and lessens our ability to make strong decisions. When we overthink, it allows us to raise doubts, which wastes time, and it also makes us lose confidence that we won't make the right decision. If you're someone who suffers from overthinking, try setting yourself a time limit to make a decision and also do what you can to become a person of action. None of us will ever make the right decision in every single scenario, but being in action is far more productive than being stuck imprisoned by your thoughts and crippled by inertia.

There is a voice that doesn't use words—listen to it

Gail Becker's story is one I'm sure every entrepreneur wishes they could write for themselves. Gail founded CAULIPOWER in mid-2016 and launched in February 2017, in an effort to fill a void she'd identified in the gluten-free food market. Gail's two sons were diagnosed with celiac disease at a young age, and after years of time-consuming workarounds at home, trying to find solutions that they liked, Gail was left with subpar results and two hungry kids.

"Despite my efforts back in those days to find nutritious solutions for my boys, I always seemed to fall short," Gail told me. "Through extensive research and trawling through Pinterest, I'd discovered hundreds of thousands of recipes for cauliflower crust pizza. Yet, making them was time-consuming, they didn't look great, and my kitchen turned upside down in the process!"

Indifferent to Gail's herculean efforts and messy kitchen, the boys loved the pizza and asked for it again. "I said no because it took ninety minutes and energy that I didn't have after coming home from a long day at the office. As an alternative, I promised I would buy it for them, but I couldn't find it anywhere. That's when I realized that this could be a viable business.

I suppose I also just got tired of all the junk such as sugar, fat, and salt that the industry kept putting into gluten-free food. I figured that if I was going through this same problem, then there were likely thousands more who were also experiencing it. So, I left my job and got to work. My mission was to reinvent food, one healthy meal hack at a time."

Gail's prior career was in journalism and public relations. She'd never worked in the food industry before, but this didn't deter her. "On my first ever sales call for CAULIPOWER I took my two sons with me because I wanted them to see that you can always make a change in your life. I am always telling them that if you don't bet on yourself, who will?"

Gail's rise to success has been nothing short of meteoric. In less than two years after launching, CAULIPOWER ranked as America's eighth top-selling pizza brand out of a universe of 500. The company also entered three new categories by giving long-overdue nutritional makeovers to coated chicken tenders and tortillas and introducing a bread replacement using frozen roasted sweet potato slices.

At time of print, Gail's company was on track to post revenues of more than $100 million for 2019. Her 2017 revenues were just $5 million. That's an extraordinary feat for a business based on a hunch that traditional food companies were missing a huge shift in consumer opinion and behaviors and that things could ultimately be done better.

You know all those things you've always wanted to do? You should go do them

I'm a big believer in gut instinct and have largely been led by intuition in everything I do. That's not to say I don't consider other factors, but for the most part, the decisions I've made have been dictated by what feels right.

Vibes don't lie. When a decision is the right one to make, you get tingles up your arms. Your tummy starts to feel a little funny. You can feel your heart rate climb a few notches.

Many years ago, a woman named Dani approached me after one of our Melbourne events. She introduced herself and wasted no time getting to her point. "Do you have a magazine for your members?" she asked. I wasted no time getting to mine: "We don't, but I'd love one."

I had no publishing experience, and I didn't have the numbers or data to see how this could work, but I got a really good feeling from this woman, and that was enough for me. I sensed we'd work well together, and with every cell in my body saying, "Go for it!" I agreed to meet with her later that month to get started.

I'm so grateful that I listened to my gut that day. It meant I got to work with Dani to create *Latte*, our magazine, which is still going strong ten years later. And as an added bonus, Dani has gone on to become one of my closest girlfriends in the world and one of my most trusted advisors.

You don't have to finish everything you start

There's no doubt that big decisions you're emotionally invested in are hard to make. It's also often harder to stop doing something than it is to start. Think about the relationships you've wanted to exit, and the jobs you've wanted to leave.

I'll never forget the day that ultimately led to me dropping out of university. I'd started a business degree, but after six months, I was feeling disillusioned. I could see the end game—a degree—but the process made no sense to me.

I'd drive forty minutes to get to university, then spend twenty minutes trying to find a parking space, take another fifteen minutes to walk to the campus, and by the time I got there, I already felt I'd wasted a bunch of time. Each day, I'd battle the crowds of students, only to get into a big, cold lecture theater with an uncharismatic lecturer who espoused the teachings of some textbook that had been written at least twenty years prior. As each day passed, I could see a long three years ahead and started questioning if this was the best use of my time.

> ## If you always do what you've always done, you always get what you've always gotten.
> ### JESSIE POTTER

My university was in North Sydney, so I had to cross the Sydney Harbour Bridge each day. It was back at a time when there were toll booths on the bridge, so you'd slow down, drive up to the booth, and hand two dollars to the poor collector who got paid to sit there all day.

After one particularly dreary day (learning about some management philosophy by some teacher who had never run a business), I approached the bridge on the way home and fumbled in my bag for the two dollars. I could place my hand on a fifty-cent coin, and a twenty-cent coin, but there was nothing more. I looked in all the compartments of my car and handbag, a search that usually returned a few more dollars in coins, but this time resulted in nothing. I don't remember what happened next—I guess they would have sent me a fine in the mail, or perhaps they took pity on me and just let me through—but I spent that whole trip driving home saying to myself, "Something's gotta change, something's gotta change."

I didn't have the answer for what I'd do if I dropped out of university, but I knew that I wanted to make something of myself. I also knew that staying at university wasn't going to do that for me. I got the sense that I wasn't going to learn in a lecture theater as fast as I could in the real world. So, on that day, when I couldn't afford the two dollars to cross the Sydney Harbour Bridge, I decided to trust my gut and never go back. And it was one of the best things I ever did.

GETTING AHEAD

"One day I was at home in Sydney, Australia, and I was writing a review of a Helmut Lang show off the Internet, and I remember feeling that I didn't want to see this secondhand. I wanted to see it for myself. That was the moment for me where I just knew I had to go—there wasn't even a choice. So I packed up my life and moved to New York with one suitcase and $5,000 in my bank account.

I didn't have a job, but I did have a few contacts, and I just put one foot in front of the other. I knew I had the equity of my experience, and I had to trust that knowledge would always support me. Eighteen years later, I'm still here! Overthinking, to me, is fatal. Trust yourself, and get it done."

LAURA BROWN
Editor in chief, *InStyle* magazine

A FEW EXTRA MILES

The people who make it to the top—whether they're musicians, or great chefs, or corporate honchos—are addicted to their calling ...

QUINCY JONES

Most people believe that work takes energy away from you, that it's just a means to an end. That it's something we have to do. You work, you get paid. End of story.

I'd like to offer an alternative to this: that when your work is what you want to be doing, it will give you energy and be a healthy addiction that you want to keep fueling.

I draw an abundance of inspiration from artists who are unapologetically passionate and obsessed with what they do. The non-artists may call these types divas—the Lady Gagas, Beyoncés, and Whitney Houstons—but I call them extraordinary. They're so sure of what they want, and so deeply connected to getting it right, that they'll do whatever it takes to perfect their craft and go where others haven't gone before.

In *Gaga: Five Foot Two*, the documentary chronicling Lady Gaga's life around the time of her 2017 Super Bowl performance, we learn just how serious Gaga is about getting it right. During one rehearsal, she emphatically addresses her team about what is and isn't working and discovers the lining of a jacket has been changed. She politely but firmly tells the wardrobe assistant to change it back. "This is the stuff that's making me nervous. I know to other people it's like 'Oh no big deal. It's just the lining of a jacket.' But for me, the way the fabric reacts to this fabric, is going to change the speed in which my arm enters the sleeve."

Is there anything more inspiring than someone who is exceptionally talented showing such deep passion about their work? I think not.

I've always seen my work as a form of art, if you will. It's my masterpiece. It never really escapes me, nor do I want it to. My work is not something I run away from at the first available opportunity. I think about it when I'm asleep. I think about it when I'm driving, when I'm in the shower, when I'm feeding the baby. And there's nothing wrong with that. It's how I express myself, and it's one of the big ways I want to make an impact in this one short life I've been given.

You don't have to be the boss of a business to have this mentality. I've seen it exist in so many of my team members over the years, and in my experience, it's these people who are among the happiest and most fulfilled I've met.

When I was eighteen and fresh from quitting university, I met a woman at a party who had just started a small recruitment company. She asked what I was doing, and I told her that I had been studying business and wanted to major in human resources, but that I hated university and had just dropped out. She then told me that she and her business partner were looking to hire someone.

I immediately felt drawn to the opportunity (let's be honest—I had absolutely no other options in front of me), and when she told me they were looking to pay $38,000, my heart skipped a beat. I was eighteen, and I was going to be rich!

We agreed to meet up in a week, and the interview turned out to be more like a chat between old friends. A few days later, she called and offered me the role. I happily accepted (hello, $38,000!) and went in to collect the paperwork. On the way home, I stopped at my favorite café to look through it all.

It was all pretty standard, but when I got to the employment contract, it listed the salary at $24,000. It was like I'd been kicked in the gut. In fairness, we'd never talked about money apart from that first time we'd met. I guess she and her business partner talked about the young woman with zero experience and they'd agreed on a new amount, which was altogether fair enough.

After a deflated minute, I picked myself up and put on my "I'll show you" attitude, which is the attitude that's pretty much got me through life so far. I decided then and there to make myself invaluable and irreplaceable. I'd do whatever it took to prove myself and to prove my worth.

It's never crowded along the extra mile.
WAYNE DYER

When I started the job, enthusiasm was pretty much all I had. Luckily for me, I had an endless supply. Originally, it was just the two business owners, an assistant, and me. I'd be the first person in the office every single day and the last one to leave at night. I'd answer the phone with a big smile and greet visitors like they were old friends. I'd clean out the trash cans with an unreasonable sense of satisfaction and collect the lunch like there was no more important task in the world. It was also my job to type up résumés, manage the one inbox we had, and run to the bank to deposit checks. You name it, I did it.

I systemized all our documentation so that it was all in the same size typeface and the tone was welcoming. I saw that the walls in the office weren't the same color as our logo, so I asked my dad to come in and help paint them to match. I was well and truly making most of this stuff up on the fly (my first real life lesson in winging it), but I knew how to treat people, and I knew how to be kind, and most important, I cared.

No one ever asked me to do any of this, but they didn't complain when I took initiative either. Truth be told, I loved being useful and making an impact. I found business exhilarating. I would work six days a week, sometimes fifteen hours a day, and I didn't mind one bit. The term "work/life balance" didn't exist yet, and I just stopped working when I felt tired, or tried something new when I got bored. It all felt a little bit more organic and easier back then. To me, there was no delineation between work and life—wasn't this all just living? To be designing a future I loved, to be learning, to be progressing, and to be educating myself—that was living large to me then and still is today.

"Hustle beats talent when talent doesn't hustle."

ROSS SIMMONDS

Shortly after I started, one of the company's two business partners was having second thoughts about being in a start-up. He had built up big personnel companies for the best part of the previous thirty years, and I guess he was just tired by that stage. He agreed that he would exit and hand the reins to his partner. I don't know the terms of that deal. We were so tiny at that point. There was probably no cash to speak of and no real value of any sort, so it's likely they just gave each other a hug and parted ways. As he finished that meeting, he turned around and said, "If you were going to offer equity in this business to anyone, you should offer it to that young kid sitting there," pointing directly at me.

So that's how I found myself as an eighteen-year-old university dropout, now a shareholder in a little recruitment business. That little recruitment business went on to become an award-winning agency with a brilliant culture, prestigious clients, and a fantastic team leading the way. A huge stroke of luck for me maybe, but you make your own luck, right?

The ambition drought

I believe that too many people are simply not willing to run the extra mile these days. We're drowning in entitlement, choking on mediocrity, and dying from apathy one workplace at a time.

While the whole work/life balance conversation has given us a lot, I think that if it's poorly managed, it can feed an entitlement culture. By encouraging an "attain work/life balance or die" philosophy, the artists, the dreamers, and the doers are not fulfilling their potential because of a rule that says you can't possibly be healthy if you're still at your desk after 5:00 p.m.

Everyone's more stressed than we've ever been, and yet many businesses have never been more accommodating to flexibility and perks. It's something I find difficult to get my head around, and I can't help but think we're getting it a little wrong. We've become so obsessed with work/life balance that somewhere along the way, we've made it uncool to work hard.

> Instead of wondering when your next vacation is, maybe you should set up a life you don't need to escape from.
>
> **SETH GODIN**

Of course, our employers have a responsibility to build cultures that encourage this level of passion, and they must reward their team members fittingly. It's a two-way street, with companies having to work just as hard when it comes to meeting the needs of their people.

To get ahead, you might have to spend a couple of hours on a Sunday night organizing yourself for the upcoming week. You may have to occasionally skip your lunchtime SoulCycle class to meet a deadline. If you hate your job, of course that's going to be a problem. But I wholeheartedly believe that if you love what you do, you'll do these things without thinking twice. They won't feel like work.

Striving for more in your career doesn't make you a workaholic. There's a distinction here. The ambitious, hardworking people I have around me know when to switch off and feel no guilt around this. They know they're committed and they know they get results. When the rosé comes out, they've earned it, and they enjoy it. They self-regulate because that's what being a grown-up is. They manage their time well, and they're rewarded with the flexibility they need to live their lives and love their work. With cooperation between employer and employee, the two can coexist.

Some of the most content people I know are the ones who have found purpose in their work. They don't watch the clock every day so they can race home to watch the latest episode of *Game of Thrones*. They don't have to be coerced into staying late when a deadline is looming, and they'll happily reply to the occasional email at 3:00 p.m. on a Saturday because there's an opportunity and they want to jump on it. They have an attitude of "it's cool, it's part of the job, whatever it takes."

These people are inspiring to work alongside each day. They believe you can love your job, work hard, and get all your other needs met too.

They show up every day with a smile on their face, committed to putting good work out in the world. They believe that if you work hard and have a great team by your side, it's possible to achieve almost anything, particularly if the lining of your jacket is perfect.

WHAT SUCCESSFUL PEOPLE DO DIFFERENTLY

Be so good they can't ignore you.
STEVE MARTIN

A few years back, I mentored an ambitious young woman, Courtney, who was fresh out of college and ready to take over the world. I loved my catch-ups with Courtney. In lots of ways, she reminded me of myself at that age. I've always found I get more from mentoring others than I get from being mentored. Lots of the lessons I heard myself imparting to Courtney were filled with advice I still needed to be reminded of too. Through the teaching, I found myself learning.

I'll never forget how, at one of our first meetings, Courtney bounded into the café, sat down, whipped out a notepad, flipped it open, took a breath, and asked her first question, which was written at the top of the page: "How do I become successful?"

She picked up her pen, eagerly awaiting my reply, as if that question could be answered in thirty seconds or less.

A little floored by the confidence of young Courtney, I stammered out a bit of a half-assed response (which she seemed perfectly satisfied with), but I remember going home that night and contemplating the question further. What really separates the good people from the successful people and the successful people from the mega-successful?

I reckon it comes down to a few key things.

THEY'RE NOT AFRAID OF VULNERABILITY. The world has woken up to the idea that, if you'd like to be successful at work and in your relationships, you should have a go at being vulnerable (thanks mostly to Dr. Brené Brown, whose TED Talk, with over forty-six million views, brought the notion that success requires vulnerability into the spotlight).

Brené encourages us to see that vulnerability is not a sign of weakness but actually a measure of strength, and she says that it's a skill that can be mastered.

I have a call with a business coach every week, and it's a rare session when a box of Kleenex isn't required. I love the chance to truly open up and express where I'm stuck and how I'm feeling, even when it mostly means I'm reduced to a blubbering mess.

You'd expect to feel safe in a session with a coach or therapist—it's their job to make you feel that way, after all—but you also have to be willing to do the work of being vulnerable. It's easy to put on a mask and pretend that everything's perfect. It takes a lot more strength to reach in and admit, "I'm not 100 percent coping here." The same amount of effort is required in your workplace and in your relationships, where vulnerability is the bridge to the connection we so deeply crave.

You'll know your workplace has a supportive culture if you feel safe admitting you don't have the answer at times. I can't imagine a world where everyone has to walk around giving the impression that they have it all together every single day.

As Brené says, "Courage starts with showing up and letting ourselves be seen." Whenever I'm brave enough to get vulnerable and go deep with a team member, they've returned that openness to me, and we get to the truth a lot quicker.

Recently, a team member asked me for some parenting advice, saying she was struggling with the demands of raising her first child and managing her workload too. Even though we're a flexible and highly supportive workplace, our people are human, and like you'll find with any new parent, the juggle is real. When we sat down, it felt like she just wanted some reassurance and was expecting a pep talk full of pleasantries such as, "Oh, it's fine, you'll be okay, it's totally normal."

> You're not a mess. You're brave for trying.
> **UNKNOWN**

I decided a long time ago that I couldn't be a role model for my people without telling the truth. So instead of offering platitudes and a bunch of parenting tips, I shared with her how I often stumble and how I also find it completely overwhelming at times. My being vulnerable with her created the space for us to connect more deeply and show her she wasn't alone. It was way more powerful than any parenting tip I could offer.

At the end of 2017, Thankyou Group cofounder and managing director Daniel Flynn released a statement about his company's financial performance that year.

The open letter, published on the group's website, was called "Better Before Bigger," and in it, Daniel described the growing pains his business was experiencing. While they'd achieved many of their goals, a lot hadn't gone according to plan.

A new product launch had cost double the money and taken double the time they'd initially anticipated. Their core product, bottled water, had lost shelf space in supermarkets. Much-needed upgrades to their systems took a back seat to more urgent problems. An investment in a new venture had failed.

In the end, Daniel announced that they'd made the tough decision to stop producing one of their product lines. "There's a wise saying that goes, 'Anything is possible, but not everything.' So after learning a lot of lessons this year, we had to choose the areas we're going to give our all to and win in," he wrote.

What I loved about this post was the vulnerability Daniel showed. He could have blamed the competitive market conditions or the rising price of ingredients, but none of that got a mention. He owned up to their mistakes and admitted they could have done better, and in doing so, he gave us all permission to do the same.

THEY'RE FOREVER LEARNING. I've been around a lot of successful people, and they all have two blindingly obvious traits in common: they're curious, and they commit to learning all they can on the topics that interest them most. These people may not have always taken the linear path in conventional education (Dell's founder, Michael Dell, and Twitter's cofounder, Evan Williams, are famous college dropouts), but they're insatiably curious and not afraid to question their way into the unknown.

> You wouldn't let your schooling
> interfere with your education.
> **GRANT ALLEN**

Warren Buffett is the world's most successful investor, with a net worth of over $87 billion. Buffett is ninety and has devoted his life to learning, estimating that he has spent 80 percent of his career reading and thinking.

In 2016, Charlie Munger, Buffett's business partner of forty years, shared that the only scheduled appointment in Buffett's calendar one week was a haircut, and that most of his weeks were similar. While most people are running around and filling their time with meetings, deadlines, and other minutiae, Buffett can be found reading endless piles of newspapers, investment reports, and company documents.

Buffett's bestie Bill Gates famously takes time out twice a year for what he calls "think weeks." Gates heads to a remote place and spends this time alone, reading as many books as he can for up to fifteen hours a day, studying trends, and contemplating his next set of moves. The productivity from these think weeks is infamous around the corridors of Microsoft. In the days when Gates was operational in the business, he'd churn out reams of notes, ideas, and questions, and feed them back to the business for actioning.

Perhaps that's how Bill Gates and Warren Buffett came to be two of the richest people in the US. Of course, not everyone has the means to travel the world for think weeks or invest most of their waking moments in reading the papers, but there's an undeniable link between immersing yourself in learning and becoming successful.

THEY STAY ACCOUNTABLE. On the topic of open-heart surgery, very few are quick to give advice. But when it comes to business, everyone from your great-uncle to the recent graduate you met who has aspirations of becoming a famous blogger are happy to share their two cents' worth. While these people are undoubtedly well-meaning, it's important to take your lead from those who have actually been in the trenches for some time.

When I was just starting out in business, I was obsessed with learning and getting my hands on as much new information as I could. I'd devour one or two business books a week. A friend saw how enthusiastic I was, so suggested I join a peer-to-peer business network for entrepreneurs. Suddenly, I found myself surrounded by people who knew loads more than I did. These people quickly became trusted advisors and mentors, and it changed the course of my life (not least because this was where I met my future husband!).

Over time, what I came to value more than their mentorship and advice was how accountable they kept me. Whenever I voiced a dream or a goal, they didn't let me get away with just airing it. Somehow, that dream or goal, now shared with these friends, became their responsibility too—they'd have to play a part in keeping me accountable. I returned the responsibility, never letting them get away with not being true to their word.

I loved the discipline and the firm approach to getting things done. Mentors and advisors are great, but the relationship often ends at the start of where you really need it to: keeping you answerable, without

"If you're the smartest person in the room,
you're in the wrong room."

UNKNOWN

excuses or blame. My peers and I spoke in a language that might have been too direct for some, but if you were going for real results like we all were, communicating this way worked. Sentences started with, "Yeah, but you said you were going to . . . " followed up by, "But none of that matters. Why haven't you done it yet?"

When I didn't complete a task that I'd promised to, I felt I'd let the team down, and it only fueled me to do better by the next time we got together.

This accountability cycle ushered me into a new level of personal leadership and focus. I was always pushing myself, asking for feedback, and wanting to do the best job I could.

Too often we surround ourselves with people who won't stretch us as much as we could be stretched. It's much easier and more comfortable to only have friends telling us, "You're amazing!" but there's far more value in surrounding ourselves with people who'll say, "You're capable of more, and I'm here to remind you of that."

THEY SEEK FEEDBACK. In my opinion, there are two types of people in the world: those who genuinely want to improve and will do whatever it takes and, well, those who don't.

Doing whatever it takes to improve starts with being open to feedback. It's being receptive to others' opinions of you, whether you like it or not, and it's having the courage to sit with that feedback, then deciding how to take action.

Early on in my career, I got into the lame habit of wearing the same thing each day (hey, Mark Zuckerberg does it!), partly because it was easier (I didn't have to think about it each morning), and partly because I'd convinced myself that the chambray shirt with our logo on it was good for business. Cringe. A mentor told me I should stop wearing "the uniform" and also get a haircut so I'd look a little older. At first, I'll admit, I was a little offended ("What's wrong with chambray?"), but I accepted her feedback, stopped wearing those shirts, and lost the ponytail too. I was twenty, and she was forty-five. She was looking in. I couldn't see out.

People who are closed to feedback can be very hard to be around. It's as if you're always walking on eggshells and hesitant to say anything because you don't know how it's going to land with them. They can also be smug and arrogant and give off an air of being better than anyone else. How the heck can you improve if your walls are up and people feel scared to tell you what they think? There's usually a reason why these people are hypersensitive. It's either because of an acute lack of confidence or because they genuinely believe they know better than anyone else.

My favorite people to work with are the ones who are coachable and know that I'm sharing feedback only to help them get better (in the same way I hope they'd return the favor to me!). You want to make sure you build a reputation as someone who is coachable because, quite frankly, no one wants to work with people who are so closed that they don't feel they can do any better.

These days, I'm constantly asking for feedback from people whose opinions I respect. Whenever I do a speaking gig, I always ask the client how I did. I want them to tell me honestly about what worked and what didn't. After every single event we produce, I always call my CEO and ask her how it was on a scale of one to ten. I'm interested in how we can improve for next time and what the takeaways were, even if it can be hard to hear at times. I'm always asking my kids for feedback, too, on what it would take for me to be a better mother. The answer usually ranges from the unhelpful, "You should give us more ice cream," to the encouraging, "Nothing, you're the best mom in the world." Mostly, these answers will be predictable and expected, but every now and then a gem will fall out and cause you to think a little harder.

At our core, we all just want to know if we're improving and getting better. The progress need not be in leaps and bounds, but it's got to be enough to convince us to keep going.

TIME-SAVING HACKS

If there's one thing I loathe, it's wasting time. There's nothing worse to me than sitting idle or using time inefficiently. I'm always one of the last people to get on the plane (why would you want to sit there for more time than you have to?), and if I'm in a meeting with my team and we're just having a talk fest, I'll be the one to interrupt and get us back on track.

I'm constantly getting asked how I fit thirty hours into twenty-four, so here you have it. My favorite time-saving hacks. You're welcome.

DO IT NOW. I try to never handle emails twice. When I read an email, I try to respond then and there and delete it. I don't open it, read it, close it, and go back to it another time.

DONE IS BETTER THAN PERFECT. I gave up perfectionism a long time ago. I'm all about doing a quality job, but there are always corners to be cut.

SHORTER EMAILS ARE BETTER. Effective writing is actually saying what you need to say in as few words as possible. Often the fewer words, the greater the impact. There are few things more disrespectful than someone sending an email that goes on for days. No one has that time.

NO EMAILS ARE BETTER YET. Do you really need to send it? Can you shout out across the office? Or get up and actually talk to someone? Pick up the phone?

OUTSOURCING IS WHERE IT'S AT. I get groceries delivered. When a kid gets sick, I use a telemedicine app where you dial up a doctor and have a video consult over your phone, and then they send the prescription to your closest pharmacy. No more doctors' waiting rooms for me! If you can bring the world to you, you'll save on precious time.

DUMP THE MEETINGS. Ineffective meetings are the bane of my existence. I'll do anything to avoid them. The conversation generally expands to the time you have available, and so much time is wasted. Meetings should be for meaningful decision-making and moving the game forward. Whenever I get asked to be in a meeting, my response is, "Does this really need to be a meeting?" and "Do you really need me?" If it's critical, I'll do it, but I much prefer a quick conversation or, even better, a walk and talk around the block.

DO THE WORST FIRST. My willpower is highest in the morning, so I tackle the hardest thing first. When it's out of the way, it makes me feel good, and feeling good propels me to want to achieve more.

MAKE EVERYTHING A GAME. When I was little, I'd play a game with my sister whenever we had to do the washing up. I'd look at the time and tell her, "Okay, let's get this done by 7:24 p.m.," and we'd race to beat the clock. Nothing's really changed. I still set myself little races all day long. "Let's get this pitch in by 12:00 p.m.," "Let's get to inbox zero by 2:15 p.m.," and so on. It makes me extraordinarily focused and means no time is wasted. Ready, set, go!

DELEGATE. There are loads of reasons why people don't delegate: thinking they don't have the time to train someone else, the fear of losing control, a concern that someone else will get the credit, that they'll lose the jobs they actually enjoy, that they can do it better, or that they don't trust others to do a satisfactory job.

These reasons are all valid, but unless you find a way through them, nothing will change. The first step is accepting that yes, others probably won't do it as well as you, and they'll most likely do it differently. Big deal. The aim here is not perfection—the aim is to save time. If you're worried about losing control or giving someone else the credit, then you're managing from ego, and that's never the best way to lead. Seek joy in watching others achieve a task that was once yours. You're giving a gift of empowerment, and that's a beautiful thing.

SIT ON YOUR HANDS. There was a time, when I knew no better, that I volunteered to be class parent. It was the first time I'd ever had a child at school, so I was full of enthusiasm and had no idea what the role entailed or what I was doing. The lovely kindergarten teacher looked straight at me when she said, "Okay, who's going to volunteer to be class parent?" I just couldn't help myself! It was definitely one of those times I should have sat on my hands and said nothing. Those class parents need medals for all they do. I fumbled my way through for the first term and failed miserably. I struggle enough to get my own kids in their sports uniforms on the right day, let alone remind everyone else to do the same. Thank goodness the other class parent was both forgiving and exceptional at the job, so she stepped up, but it was a great lesson in overcommitment for me.

PICK WHAT YOU'RE GOOD AT. While I'm useless at admin, you can always count on me to be there with class supplies or be the one to buy a great present on behalf of everyone for the teacher. It's important for everyone to play to their strengths (more on that soon!).

CONTROL YOUR ENVIRONMENT. I choose carefully what I read and what information I absorb. I rarely watch television. In fact, the only TV in our entire house is in our bedroom (I know, right now you're wondering how we ever managed to make six babies). I've never bought and seldom read magazines, and I don't read the news every day either. I don't spend a lot of time on social media, and it's safe to say that I completely suck at Facebook. I'll go there maybe once a week if something draws me in, but I don't spend a lot of time worrying about what other people are up to. I remember a few years back when my assistant, Britt, logged in to my Facebook account. As a committed millennial and social media user, she was aghast that I had over 280 friend requests just sitting there. Instagram is my one vice, and I'll be on there a few times a day. I only follow and connect with people who enrich my life, and I unfollow them if they make me feel anything other than positive.

DON'T COMMUTE. A 2015 study conducted by Canada's University of Waterloo discovered a direct correlation between commute time and well-being. The survey found that people with the longest commutes have the lowest overall satisfaction with life. I'll do almost anything I can to avoid a commute. If you can, draw a seven-mile radius around your home and try to have all your regular activities fit in that circle. Get your office in that circle, your kids' schools, and any shops you access too. Sitting in a car or on public transport is time wasted that you could spend on being productive elsewhere. If you just can't avoid a commute, use that time wisely: meditate, or get ahead with your day by planning how you're going to be effective. Take a gratitude journal with you, get a good book, do an online course while you're traveling—anything apart from just mindlessly whittling away time on social media.

BE A MULTITASKING DEMON. Science tells us not to multitask, so let's listen to that. We all get it: the tasks that require your full focus need to get your full focus. And I'm not for a second suggesting that you text and drive, or anything irresponsible like that. I am saying that if you're in the hairdresser's chair for two hours, make those two hours count. My hairdresser would fall over if I arrived without my laptop. It's never happened. I make calls on my short commute to the office (hands-free, relax), I'll feed my baby while having a chat with another of the kids, I read stories to the kids while they're in the bath, and we have a rule in my house that you're not allowed up the stairs without carrying something that needs to be put away.

BEWARE THE CHARITY COFFEE. We all get asked to have coffee and a chat. But you should be protective of your time and use it wisely. Of course, some businesses and roles require you to be out meeting new people all the time, and if this is you, go for it. If not, be ruthless with your time. The quicker you cultivate the skill of saying no and protecting your time from nonessential business, the better.

SAY NO. A LOT. I turn down lots of things that just aren't going to give me pleasure or help in any way. I guard my time above all else. It's always my number-one consideration.

CULTIVATING RELATION-SHIPS

"Stepping into the CEO role with zero experience was the biggest winging it moment for me. At the time, I was considering taking six months off to focus on getting pregnant after four years of trying and miscarrying.

In the end, I decided that life is too short and to just go for it and work it out as I went along. The worst thing that could happen was to fail and get a regular 'job' again.

Six months into the role, I got pregnant naturally, and now I have a beautiful three-year-old girl. Taking the CEO role was the best decision I've ever made, and I've definitely been 'winging it' ever since. Don't tell the boss!"

OLIVIA RUELLO
CEO, Business Chicks Australia

CARE DEEPLY

> I care. I care a lot.
> It's kind of my thing.
>
> **LESLIE KNOPE**

From a young age, I was taught to care. I mean, no one ever sat me down and said, "Em, you have to care," but I learned by watching my parents. My mom would spend hours designing and making her own holiday cards, a tradition that she'd start in early November, and diligently work on every night until she was done. She'd design eight or nine different cards each year, always asking me, my sister, and my brother what we thought of them (it was a family affair), and then she'd think carefully about who'd receive each one. Those cards have become a little bit famous in my mom's circle of friends, many of them telling me, "Oh, I've kept every one of Deb's cards for the past twenty years!"

I suppose my mom, through this task and also in the way she conducted herself in everyday life, taught me that we should make time for people and nurture them in whatever ways we can.

My dad, although trained as an accountant, would always be the first person to offer his time and handyman skills to people who needed them. He was always off fixing someone's bathroom, or building them a deck. A lot of the time he'd do this for free, or for precious little money, out of love and because he was kind.

My way of caring for people has predominantly been through the businesses I've built, as it's all I've ever known. What I've learned is that people just want to be heard, to be loved, and to feel as though they count. You can never underestimate the power a simple act of kindness can have on making someone feel like they matter.

It's no accident that my first business was a recruitment company, and now I run a business that's all about helping women get

"No act of kindness,
no matter how small,
is ever wasted."

AESOP

ahead. If you look at those businesses, they have something in common: people and relationships. The way I've grown my relationships is by giving more than I take and being persistent in that generosity. I never worry what people think about me, but I care deeply about how I make people feel.

Nothing brings me more joy than creating an experience or a memory for someone else. I've grown my businesses based on this philosophy, and I'm obsessed with finding ways to make people feel special. What can be more important than making the journey a little more gentle and a lot more fun for someone?

It might mean sending a bag of See's Candies to a friend who loves them, or sending groceries to a team member who's just moved house, or even just picking up an extra coffee for a colleague on my way into the office.

One time, I jumped at the chance to make the day of one of our members. I'd never met Bernadette, but my team had told me she was a huge fan of Sir Bob Geldof and was flying to hear him speak at a Business Chicks event. When Bernadette walked into the room on the day of the event, I was ready and waiting, directing her straight to her seat at the VIP table, right next to Sir Bob. I didn't do it for any ulterior motive. I didn't need anything from Bernadette; the look on her face was all the thanks anyone could have asked for. That's what kindness is: doing these things just because.

How to make people feel special

It's not hard to be kind to people; in fact, it's often quite easy to make someone's day. Here are some simple ways to make the people around you feel special.

PERSONALIZE EVERYTHING. When I got married ten years ago, I wanted the experience to be amazing for the guests. They were our most treasured friends and family, after all, and I wanted them to know how much they were loved. So, I created a handwritten card for every single guest and placed it in a beautiful gift box on their place settings. People were in tears when they read them. Sure, it took me a lot of time to craft these messages for so many people, but the impact it created was worth the effort.

IF YOUR PARTNER TRAVELS, LEAVE NOTES IN THEIR SOCKS AND THROUGHOUT THEIR SUITCASE. There's nothing better than arriving somewhere far from home, opening your luggage, and feeling a bit of love.

DO SOMETHING ON A HUGE SCALE. When my sister and brother-in-law got engaged, I went and bought 30 feet of fabric and made them a sign—Happy Engagement Liv and Mitch—that hung in the garden where they had their engagement party.

FOCUS ON WHAT'S IMPORTANT TO THEM. People will give you clues about what's most precious to them. (Hint: it's usually what they talk about the most.) If it's their family, then stick their photo in a frame and send it their way. If it's travel, buy a book about a place they're dying to go to.

GIVE THOUGHTFUL GIFTS. When one of our members or friends has a baby, I'll often go online and send a bunch of groceries to the new mama, curating it for her personal taste. Sure, I'll include diapers and baby wipes, but if I know she's partial to a Kit Kat or a bundle of kale, I'll add those to the cart too.

GET ORGANIZED. Systemize what you can. Grab some boxed note-cards, a nice pen, and a bunch of stamps, and have them at the ready for when someone pops into your mind and might need to receive some love.

COMPLIMENT OFTEN. Whenever I meet someone for the first time, I always try to find something to compliment them on. It might be a piece of their clothing or their smile or eyes or teeth (yep!), but I will never, ever be disingenuous. If nothing comes to me immediately, I don't make it up.

BE YOUR WORD. It's important to do what you've said you're going to do. In a world where people are constantly canceling or postponing, sometimes just committing to something is the kindest thing you can do.

REMEMBER THE DETAILS. Do what you can to remember things: names, pets, favorite foods, the city someone comes from. Instead of saying, "How's the baby?" make an effort to use the baby's name. You'll get remembered if you remember the details.

"People will forget what you said and did, but they won't forget how you made them feel." These words have become well-known over time and for good reason. While it's important to be prepared and know your content (whether you're giving a speech or just attending a meeting), it matters more how you deliver your message and how you conduct yourself.

And my one rule for a life well-lived? Never be the first person to leave a hug.

SHOW UP AND SMILE

Over the years, I've seen firsthand how celebrities and business personalities conduct themselves. I'll go to my grave with some of the secrets I've collected and won't name names, but I'll also never forget the behavior of one well-known media identity at one of our events.

She arrived late, completely disinterested and dismissive of everyone she came into contact with. You could tell she didn't want to be there and she thought it beneath her to have to do what we were asking of her (which was to represent her company in front of a large group of women who looked up to her and were eager for her advice). When she got to the green room, she sighed heavily, plonked herself down on one of the couches, and lay back with her legs spread along the floor. She never stopped checking her phone. She conducted herself with such arrogance that everyone else in the room left immediately, and this attitude continued when she took to the stage.

Energy is contagious, for good or for bad. This woman only did herself a disservice by being so arrogant and rude, and she lost a lot of respect that day.

You compare that to our events with actress and activist Deborra-Lee Furness, who couldn't have been more interested or more dedicated to what she'd committed to with Business Chicks. Deb was present, maintained eye contact, showed a huge amount of interest in our work, and gave her all. She stayed after her speeches and spoke with everyone, giving them her time and full attention. To this day, we still have members talk about their experience with Deb and how much she impacted them, and this is a testament to the person and professional she is.

For years, I went and gave speeches (mostly unpaid), sat on panels, went to colleges and schools to mentor the students, and volunteered my time wherever I could. I did it all with professionalism and enthusiasm, always. I'd prepare, and I'd be on time (a teensy bit early even, but not too much, as that's often just as rude as being late). I'd be polite and present with everyone, and I'd always thank the organizers for the opportunity, making sure I sent them a note or a card afterward. In short, I'd act like I was Beyoncé being paid whatever Beyoncé gets paid to perform at one of her sold-out stadium concerts.

No matter what the task, project, or event, or what you're getting paid, it's important to show up like you're being paid a million dollars and that there's no more important job for you at that minute.

These rules don't just apply to speakers or celebrities. The way you show up in your workplace each day matters too. There's a sign at the front door of the Business Chicks office that reads, "Please take responsibility for the energy you bring into this space." It's a beautiful reminder that we're all responsible for our own mood, no matter what's going down.

A good mood and enthusiasm mean a lot, and stability also can't be overestimated. We've all had a coworker or even a boss who we've not been able to entirely predict, where we're not sure if we'll be met with a big smile or an outburst of some kind. I never want to be that leader.

When you have kids (especially when you have enough to make an entire basketball team, like I do), you learn to manage on precious little sleep. Each night, I go to sleep in one bed and wake up in another, or if I stay in the same bed, I usually wake up with one or two kids in the bed next to me. All of this means that I'm always tired, but I never let it dictate my mood. I get up, and I show up. I walk into my office every day with my shoulders back and a big smile on my face (coffee helps). I'm friendly and interested. You'll rarely hear me complain about being tired, and I try to set an example wherever I am.

Setting an example and always being in a positive mood takes effort for most people, myself included. It's true that you get to choose how you feel, even though on some days it's easier to choose to feel positive than others.

If you're in a funk and can't seem to get out of it, here are some proven scientific techniques that might help.

ACTIVATE SEROTONIN. Serotonin is the hormone that contributes to feelings of well-being and happiness. A great way to stimulate serotonin when you're not on your game is to look back over past positive memories or achievements. This might be reading an article about a time you won an award or looking through photos of a trip you took with friends. It might mean heading back in time a little and flicking through old photos of happier days on Instagram or Facebook. Try this. It really works!

TURN UP THE MUSIC AND DANCE. Or if that sounds altogether weird, just take a walk around the block, throw a ball with your dog, or climb the stairs three or four times. Calling on endorphins to help get you out of a funk is always a good idea. While movement is the best way to activate endorphins (also known as the happy hormones), there are other ways to release this critical mood-enhancing chemical. You

"It's nice to be important, but more important to be nice."

SIR JOHN MARKS TEMPLETON

could have some chocolate or have a drink. Alcohol is a great way to release endorphins—of course, we all know alcohol is not the long-term solution to combating bad moods, but in moderation, go for it! Sex is a great way to release endorphins. Laughter is, too, so call someone you know who will give you a really good belly laugh. Even just the act of smiling releases endorphins. It has also been reported that vanilla and lavender scents can stimulate this hormone—who knew? A somewhat counterintuitive way to release endorphins is to have a good cry as well. Breaking down and releasing emotions is a wonderful way to become instantly more relaxed and feel a sense of relief.

VISUALIZE. Turning your thinking to a positive event that hasn't happened yet—an upcoming vacation or a big fat goal you want to achieve—does wonders for your dopamine levels (another hormone that's great for tackling bad moods). If you're in a funk, get a stack of magazines, cut out pictures of things that you want to bring into your life, and stick them up on a big bit of cardboard. *Voilà!* A vision board! A friend of mine did this years ago, pinning up a picture of an apartment with water views that took his fancy. Four years later, he moved house. While he was unpacking, he found his old vision board in one of the boxes. Right there was the advertisement he had cut out and pinned up for the exact same apartment that he had just bought and moved into. Not the one to the left or the right, but the exact same apartment! You can't make this stuff up!

If a vision board doesn't sound like your thing, grab a pen and piece of paper and write out your bucket list. Spend a moment planning for how you're going to tick off an item or two from that list. Remember, little steps count here so just take one or two actions toward achieving an item on your bucket list.

Even just putting your vision board or your bucket list somewhere that you walk past each day (instead of hiding it in your closet) has a way of bringing these goals closer to you.

EARN TRUST

A few years ago, a friend asked me to come along to a party for a "surprise guest." My friend was well connected, so it could've been anyone. For weeks, I wondered who the mystery person could be, and it had me stumped and distracted.

The party was held at a boutique hotel, the kind that you could rent out for a night or the weekend if your budget allowed. It had a restaurant and bar at the front, and at the back there were two apartments separated by a pool that looked like something straight out of the Playboy Mansion. It was supremely cool, the kind of place rock bands and movie stars chose to stay when they came to town.

I knocked on the door, and a burly security guard answered. He greeted me and asked if I'd mind handing him my phone. Back then, social media didn't exist, and our phones didn't even take photos anyway, but I'd been told we needed to be discreet, so I happily passed it over.

The security guard took me through to the back of the uber-chic venue, and it was all quite understated, with only about fifteen people there. After a while, I looked up to the second level of one of the apartments, and a shadow caught my eye. The room had floor-to-ceiling glass, so I could clearly make out a silhouette. The person turned toward the light, and I recognized him immediately. Booyah, Bill Gates!

I'm a business junkie so it probably won't surprise you that I was pretty stoked about the mystery guest lottery I'd just won. Throughout the evening, I watched as everyone fawned over him ("What can I get you, Bill?" "Oh my goodness—I can't believe you're here and I'm meeting you!") and generally made a huge fuss over him. I decided not to do any of that and instead used the night as a mini social experiment. Of course, I shook his hand and introduced myself, but I didn't try too hard; I gave lots of eye contact and a warm, genuine smile for sure, but I didn't fixate on how to impress him.

Most smart people can smell bullshit a mile off, just as they can sense authenticity. For one reason or another, Bill sensed my trustworthiness. Later in the evening, we got talking, and that conversation lasted for hours.

I asked about his wife, Melinda, and his family, and he happily opened up. He spoke about his home and which music he liked and how he had started Microsoft in his garage, recalling the days when there were just six people in the company. At the time we met, Bill had over 60,000 employees globally, and we had a good chuckle about that. He seemed genuinely surprised by his success and where it had taken him. Of course, I was curious to know more, but I never pressed for any more information about the business. It was a Saturday night, and he was there to unwind and relax, not talk shop.

Bill Gates was the first mega-successful, high-profile entrepreneur I'd spent time with. I tell this story not because I'm interested in name-dropping, but because he taught me my first important lesson about highly successful people: generally, they are just like us. While I didn't know it at the time, it was the starting point for a lot of things to come.

Since that night, I've watched this play out with the incredible businesspeople I've been able to spend time with, and the same rules apply: be present, be interested, and above all, just be yourself.

Networking done wrong

Meaningful relationship building requires a softly, softly, gentle approach. You have to know when to stop and leave people alone, and often, stopping is the best way to go. Buy some time, show that you're genuine and not a stalker, build your credibility, and reapproach when you've got something significant to share.

If you're lucky enough to meet Jamie Oliver and all you do with that time is try to pitch him your idea for a green granola bar (I've seen it happen), immediately you've put him in a difficult position of having to say yes or no. Being put on the spot is really tricky territory for an influential person. They're always walking the tightrope between wanting to be lovely and honoring the reality of having no time or being distracted by the job they need to do. You'd have more luck with Jamie if you got him talking about one of his five gorgeous kids or asked him about his latest food project.

Your little black book can be your greatest asset, if handled with care. It only takes one little mistake for you to lose credibility, so it's important to treat every relationship with the respect it deserves.

Not a week passes without me being asked to make an introduction to one of the personalities I've worked with over the years. Where I can, I'll happily do it, but the truth is that a lot of the time it's just not appropriate.

I'm a generous networker, and I will always find a way to get people what they need, but there's a point at which you cross a line and become annoying, and it can be a fine one!

Your success will skyrocket if you can master the relationship-building game. Here's how I navigate mine.

ASK WHAT'S IN IT FOR THEM. I get pitched to a lot. It might be for me to invest in a start-up or to give a speech at a function or to mentor someone who needs a leg up on their business journey. Most of these pitches fall short. To start with, they're far too long. You've got to understand your audience. I'm time-poor (I mean, who isn't?), so you need to be succinct and impactful. I will never read an email that looks like an essay, where I have to spend time searching for what's being asked.

ASK YOURSELF IF A MEETING IS REALLY NECESSARY. Think about it for a second. Do you really need to meet up in person? Sometimes you may need to give up the idea that a face-to-face meeting is required. Many times, someone has asked to see me and they've been so persistent that I've relented and booked a meeting in. I'll sit there with them and my latte for half an hour thinking, "What do you actually want?" Eventually, they'll summon the courage to get to their point and ask me a question (e.g., "Can you mentor me?" or "Will you sponsor this event?"), which they could have done over a call or an email. It leaves me feeling frustrated that my time has been wasted (and theirs too!).

IF YOU'RE REACHING OUT TO AN INFLUENTIAL PERSON, STOP TELL-ING THEM YOU'LL BUY THEM LUNCH. I'll often get approached with, "I'd love to pick your brain and take you to lunch, my treat!" Here's the thing: I can afford to pay for my lunch, and the cost for one and a half hours of my time is worth more than that. If you really want the time of someone you're trying to build a relationship with, get creative. Send a card, or even a little video, to get their attention instead. And above all, respect their time. A salad and some sparkling mineral water won't always cut it.

KEEP IT TO YOURSELF. If you're networking well, chances are you won't be able to tell anyone about it. If you've garnered the trust and respect of an influential person, it's not kosher for you to plaster that experience all over social media, as a lot of people do. Often what you see on social media is a farce, and it's easy to succumb to believing what you read and see. In my experience, real friendships and relationships are played out behind closed doors where, if you're a trustworthy per-son, you'd never let the cameras in.

The mini, many actions

While brashness can certainly work in garnering the attention of some-one you're trying to build a relationship with, it's the mini, many ac-tions that build trust. And these mini, many actions can be tedious and take time. The truth is, not many people have the patience to stay the course, knuckle down, and put in the work. A lot of us are seeking in-stant connection, and don't understand that humans aren't built that way. We're wired to suss each other out and prove that we're worth in-vesting time in.

I've always had a huge business crush on Seth Godin. As a twenty-year-old amateur entrepreneur, I devoured all of his books, dog-earing the corners and highlighting the paragraphs that spoke to me the most. I remember getting in trouble one time at New Delhi Airport for holding up the customs line; I was so transfixed by Seth's book *Purple*

Cow, I hadn't seen the line moving. When eventually a customs official ushered me on, there were about 40 feet between me and the person in front.

I'd always had the dream to bring Seth to Australia and have him share his work with the Business Chicks audience. The problem was he lived in New York, and in my experience, a lot of New Yorkers are reluctant to travel to Australia.

I started building that relationship very gently through the occasional email, birthday message, or end-of-year card, and through mutual friends who very generously helped me eventually realize the dream. I never took Seth's continual dismissals as a personal rejection. To me, "no" just meant "not now." With each no, I saw an opportunity to find more creative ways to get him to say yes.

It took eight years. When Seth eventually agreed to visit Australia for the first time, it felt that much sweeter because it had taken so long. Persistence, patience, and being genuine are the keys to building unbreakable relationships.

HOW TO NETWORK LIKE A BOSS

Networking gets a bad rap because it's misunderstood. Networking is not about trying to get something from someone or trying to impress someone so they'll buy something from you. Networking is about building trust and rapport. It's about building a friendship where, if you're doing it right, you should be doing more for the other person than they do for you, at least at the start. It's kind of like parenting—somewhat of a thankless task, but one day it will pay back dividends (or so I'm told).

It's often thought that networking is only needed when you're looking for a new job or need a new client. I believe (love it or hate it) that networking should be an ongoing task, no matter what your role or career stage. You should invest in your networking constantly, because you never know what life is going to throw at you. You never know where opportunities are lurking and how a relationship can provide a benefit until it does.

Ten years ago, I met a gorgeous woman at a health retreat. We had precious little in common. We lived in different cities. She was a mother; I wasn't. She wasn't into business; I was. And there were twenty-five years between us. On the outside, this woman had nothing to give me, and I had nothing to give her, but that didn't stop me from throwing myself in and learning as much as I could about her. By the end of the week, through Tai Chi sessions and the sharing of activated almonds, I'd found a new friend.

Over the next ten years, we kept in touch loosely through social media. One day, I discovered that her daughter was looking for a career change. One thing led to another and now her daughter is one of our most valued team members.

I could have lost touch with this woman because, at face value, we had nothing in common. What I've learned, though, is to be kind to everyone and to invest in networking without expecting an outcome.

I always get a kick out of watching how ideas manifest and relationships flourish. Over the years, Business Chicks has been responsible for thousands of connections that have turned into great professional relationships (and one personal one too! We were thrilled last year when two of our members got married! #loveislove).

Years ago now, authors Margie Warrell and Dr. Libby Weaver came along to a Business Chicks event, where they met Kristina Karlsson, founder of lifestyle brand kikki.K. Among the three of these women, there's a whole lot of wisdom and talent going on. Margie, Libby, and Kristina didn't come to that event with any sort of explicit intention, but over time they developed a friendship that would soon turn into an idea benefiting them all. Occasionally, kikki.K publishes existing books with limited-edition covers, and on a recent trip back to Australia, I was in a kikki.K store and smiled to see both Margie and Libby's latest books on the shelves there.

> # When you need a relationship, it's too late to build it.
> ## DR. LOIS FRANKEL

Like Margie, Kristina, and Libby, here's what you're going to need to know if you want to master practical networking that turns into something more.

KNOW HOW TO START. Either find someone on their own and introduce yourself or approach a group of people. When approaching a group, hover back a little and wait for a break in the conversation. Introduce yourself confidently, and let the group open up to let you in.

GET GOOD AT ANSWERING "WHAT DO YOU DO?" Use your answer to create rapport, start a conversation, say something meaningful, and appear interesting. Say why you do what you do and why you're passionate about it. If you don't love your job, include something else that you do love doing.

DON'T BE THE PERSON WHO ASKS "WHAT DO YOU DO?" Instead, try, "What are you working on at the moment?" "What are you passionate about?" "What are you reading at the moment?" or "What are you most excited about right now?" Other simple opening lines might be, "Have you been to one of these events before?" or "Have you heard the guest speaker before?"

LISTEN MORE THAN YOU SPEAK. Every great networker I know is a brilliant listener. Most people only listen to reply—they don't listen to really understand the other person. Practice listening deeply and, when you do, you'll uncover what the other person is really trying to say. When you listen deeply, you might be able to help them come up with a solution, or allay their fears, or truly help them talk through a problem they're facing. Don't obsess with how you're going to reply;

sometimes the best response is silence, so the other person can come up with their own answers.

LEARN ABOUT NLP (NEURO-LINGUISTIC PROGRAMMING). One of the most significant things I learned early in my career is the practice of NLP. One of the fundamental basics of NLP is mirroring another person's body language, posture, speed of speech, even down to the volume that they're speaking at and how fast they're breathing. It'll enhance your communication skills and subliminally make the other person more comfortable too. Ever noticed how annoying it is when you're on a deadline or stressed about something and trying to work at a rapid pace, and someone walks up to you and speaks really slowly and can't get to their point? It works conversely too. If you're calm and measured and the other person is frantic and stressed, then you're going to have a mismatch of energy. It's worth investing some time studying NLP and at least learning how to mirror well. I promise you'll see an improvement in your relationships and communication when you do.

DON'T HAND OVER YOUR BUSINESS CARD AT THE START OF A CON-VERSATION. Don't assume that someone is interested in you or that you have something in common or will want to maintain a relationship. And always ask for permission with a simple, "Would you mind if we swapped cards?"

DON'T SELL. A lot of people still think you go to a networking function to find customers immediately. Relationships built through network-ing events are just like relationships in real life—you wouldn't propose on the first date. People have to learn about you; they have to trust you. Think about networking as a marriage. First, you're introduced to someone, then you start dating and get to know each other, then you get engaged, and then you get married.

LEAVE PEOPLE WANTING MORE. People who leave you wanting more from a conversation are more likely to be remembered than the guy who will just not take your cues and shut up. You want to avoid going on and on to someone to the point where they lose interest. You'll be remembered if you offer just that little bit less than the next person and keep your listener wanting more. Just be aware of how your story is landing; if you're seeing eyes glaze over, or people looking elsewhere, it's time to wrap it up.

NEVER BE NEGATIVE. Never gossip, never whine, and never talk badly about a past employer or employee. You want to be seen as a positive, professional person who can be trusted. If someone fishes for gossip, try to deflect it with an offhand comment and move on to show you just won't be drawn into it.

KNOW HOW TO LEAVE A CONVERSATION. At networking events, you're there to meet people and get a good return on the investment of your time, which means you should try to meet as many people as possible. Just try saying, "It's been so great talking with you and I'm here to meet as many people as possible, so let's please keep in touch!"

STOP SAYING YOU'RE BAD WITH NAMES AND START TRYING. Try repeating the person's name when you first meet, straightaway ("Nice to meet you, Zoe!"). And if there's some way you can make that name stick for you, say it again ("I work with another Zoe, and she's great!"). The first key to remembering names is to stop saying you're bad at it. Instead, practice repeating the name back and make associations to help you along.

AND LASTLY, ASK FOR WHAT YOU WANT. There's an unwritten gender expectation that women are supposed to be more caring, compassionate, and cooperative than men. The problem with this assumption is that it can lead us to feel a little icky when it comes to asking for favors or asking for what we want. I'd love to see all women step out of their comfort zones and practice asking more of each other. I love it when I get asked to help and love it when women have the courage to seek that help. We need more of this!

The importance of following up

It's still surprising to me the number of people I've offered to help (maybe someone I've met on a plane or at an event) who haven't followed up afterward. If you feel an opportunity is there, make sure you go for it. Even if no specific opportunity came from your conversation, get in touch with that person and thank them for their time.

FIND THE TIME. Don't bother going to a networking event if you're not going to follow up. I block out half an hour in my calendar to follow up after I've attended an event.

BE CLEVER WITH HOW YOU GET IT DONE. I once met a woman at a conference and we started talking about our favorite children's books. She hadn't heard of the one I recommended, so after the conference I ordered it and sent it to her. She was blown away that I'd remembered and gone to that trouble, and she's become a firm friend since. It's so important to take your cues from people. If you hear someone likes a particular kind of chocolate, it's so easy to send it to them. Great networking is about being memorable and standing out.

TELL THEM WHAT THEY TAUGHT YOU. I met a woman at a networking event once and she followed up with an email saying, "Lovely to meet you and here are some things I learned from you." She bulleted a few points that were a great summary of what we'd spoken about. It made me feel good to think I'd had an impact!

NEVER ADD SOMEONE TO YOUR DATABASE WITHOUT PERMISSION. Even if they've expressed interest in your business or you've agreed to stay in touch, you should always ask if it's okay to add them to your database. And never actually use those words—no one wants to be "added to a database." Instead, explain what's in your communications and why they might like it, and ask if they'd mind if you included them.

ASK IF YOU CAN ADD THEM TO YOUR SOCIAL NETWORKS. Ask for permission to connect on LinkedIn, and when sending the invitation, make sure you add a note about why you want to add them.

HAVE A CALL TO ACTION WITH YOUR FOLLOW UP. If you're interested in having a long-term relationship, be sure to include a call to action—for example, "Hey, Sara! It was great to meet with you last night. I know we spoke about running a webinar together. Can I give you a call next Tuesday to have a chat about that?"

HANDWRITTEN TRUMPS EMAIL EVERY TIME. We should try to make the time to write notes over emails where we can. A little card in the mail shows you care, and it guarantees you'll be remembered more than someone who just shoots off an email.

RUNNING
A
BUSINESS

"After building a successful consulting business, I had to litigate my way out of a toxic partnership. And when the opportunity came for me to start again on my own, I found myself armed with a full arsenal of excuses. But my husband—who taught me to always say 'yes' when opportunity comes asking—slayed the imaginary dragons guarding the door to an exciting future by disarming them one by one. 'I don't have a business name,' was one excuse. 'Here you go,' was his reply. 'No laptop,' was the next. 'It's on its way,' he batted back. He wore me down until I had no more excuses. I had no choice but to get on with winging it.

And you know what I discovered? That for years, I had played to my strengths, exercising the same group of muscles until I was the best weightlifter in the city. But without my old team and infrastructure around me, I had to learn new skills. I had to learn to run and to throw. And it was hard; each night for weeks my body and mind ached from the unfamiliar exercise. Until one day I woke up and realized I wasn't winging it anymore. I was doing it—and doing it pretty well at that.

So when my husband died suddenly, I knew what would be required. All of the areas of our life that he used to take care of—the household budget, and maintenance, and vacations my spoiled self had ignored—were now my responsibility too. And I started by ... just starting. One bill at a time. One supplier at a time. One banker, one utility, one meeting. I. Had. To. Wing. It.

And one day—after so many nights crying myself to sleep, screaming into the darkness, 'I can't do this'— I woke up and realized I was actually doing it."

LAHRA CAREY
principal and founder of
Lahra Carey Media and Communications

THE HARD TRUTH

We live in an age where entrepreneurship is glorified. Everywhere we turn, there's a story of businesses kicking goals or being sold for a number in the hundreds of millions, lots within their infancy too. The truth is, that's only a reality for a handful of companies and concepts. In Australia, more than 60 percent of small businesses fail within three years. In the US, 20 percent fail within the first year, and after five years, only half of the businesses still exist.

I'm not for a second saying don't go for it. I want you to. We need more entrepreneurs in the world, because they create jobs and often go on to solve big social issues when governments can't. We particularly need more female entrepreneurs, especially those who might be parents themselves, as they inherently understand the demands facing working mothers and can work to shift the needle on those challenges.

I'd love for everyone to experience the thrill of getting a business off the ground. Starting a business teaches so many skills and opens up a whole new world of learning and challenge. Here's the caveat though: it can't be at the ongoing expense of the things that truly matter to you. The key word here is "ongoing."

You should expect your start-up to consume you and take you away from almost everything else in the beginning. Sacrifices need to be made initially, but there may come a time when you have to face cold, hard facts and acknowledge that it's time to stop and, ahem, give up.

I speak to lots of people who are so unhappy because of the stress their small business is causing them and their families. They're petrified of failing and they dig their heels in, unwilling to admit the truth. Every day seems like an ongoing battle, and yet these people keep waking up each morning, blindly believing that things are going to be different somehow.

And no one is willing to talk about this.

A friend reached out to me a few weeks ago in complete exasperation. "I've been doing this for three years now and haven't gotten

"One of the hardest decisions you'll
ever face in life is choosing whether
to walk away or try harder."

ZIAD K. ABDELNOUR

anywhere!" She went on to say that she was drowning in the reality of raising three young children and trying to grow her small business. We workshopped it together and the reality emerged: she just didn't have a viable business. Even if we removed the kids from the equation, no matter how hard she worked at it, the results in her business just wouldn't change. It wasn't really a business.

It's all very well to find your passion—to do what you love and love what you do—but at the end of the day, it's not always going to put food on the table. Sometimes what's required is having a really tough conversation with yourself about whether you should continue or not.

You've got two options if you've stagnated like my friend and you haven't gone anywhere. You can either decide here and now to stop what you're doing, or you can dramatically change something. If you go with option B, just make sure your business is viable first. No point losing another three years flogging a dead horse.

No one is quick to offer this advice, and few are willing to have the tough conversation. We're playing too nice and pretending that everything's going to be okay. We tell these people to have a massage, take a vacation, run a bath, or hire a sitter for an afternoon. While these tactics might work for a couple of hours, or days even, no amount of time away from your business can mask the pain that comes with this idea: it might not be working.

In my experience, these are the common reasons why small businesses fail (or should be given up on).

THEY DON'T HAVE AN OBVIOUS AUDIENCE. One of the best ways you can approach starting a business is to identify the audience you have available to you rather than focusing on what the actual product or service is. Does your best friend have a chain of stores that you might be able to put product into? Is your cousin an Instagram influencer who could help kick-start you?

The aim of the game is to get some sales happening straight out of the gate by using the audience or distribution channel that's already available to you. This is in direct opposition to the thinking that says, "I want to start a candle business," where you go out and learn how to make candles, make 200 of the darn things in your dining room, and after you've sold some to your mom and her friends, you're left with 185 and have no clue how you're going to get them out of your apartment.

If you find yourself strolling down Los Angeles's famed Melrose Avenue and see a hoard of well-dressed millennials queuing up outside a store waiting patiently for their turn to get in, you'd be forgiven for asking, "What's going on over there?"

The scene is a daily occurrence in the popular shopping precinct and is thanks to Glossier, the cult direct-to-consumer beauty brand and brainchild of entrepreneur Emily Weiss. Weiss got her start as an intern to Lauren Conrad on the television show *The Hills*, but she quickly realized that TV was not her calling and saw the limitations of being cast as a reality star. She went on to launch her own editorial beauty blog called *Into the Gloss*, in 2010. When she started her blog, Weiss worked on it every day from 4:00 a.m. to 8:00 a.m., before she'd head in to her day job. She was able to grow the blog's following to 10 million page views each month, hire a small team, and attract some corporate sponsorship for the site.

In late 2014, using the power of social media, Weiss launched her site Glossier.com, selling just four skin-care products online. Soon after the site's debut, Glossier was able to attract $8.4 million in Series A funding, but it wasn't all smooth sailing, with Weiss pitching to twelve investment groups and getting rejected eleven times. Nevertheless, she persisted, and Glossier went on to enjoy three more funding rounds resulting in over $86 million cash, with its Series D resulting in a raise of $100 million. Reports give the company a $1.2 billion valuation, making Glossier one of only a handful of female-led "unicorns" (privately held start-ups valued at over $1 billion).

Glossier has attracted a slew of celebrity fans, including Beyoncé, who launched the company's Lidstar liquid shadow at the 2018 Grammy Awards. Celebrities aside, it's the millennial crowd happy to line up on

Melrose Avenue that most contributes to the brand's ongoing success. And with more sales per square foot that an Apple store, Glossier knows it's on to something, and it's showing no signs of slowing down any time soon.

> ## Simplicity is the keynote of all true elegance.
>
> ### COCO CHANEL

I can't help but think there's something very beautiful (and obviously highly successful) in the simplicity of this brand. If you study Glossier's customer experience journey, pay lots of attention to its simple but beautiful packaging, and understand the effectiveness of such a narrow product range (there are about forty products altogether), you'll also start to marvel at how Weiss's genius lies in her straightforwardness.

Another brand rooted in simplicity is travel and lifestyle company Away. Founded in late 2015 by Stephanie Korcy and Jennifer Rubio, who met while working as executives at eyewear company Warby Parker, Away has captured the hearts (and Instagram accounts) of travelers who value style, convenience, and function.

Away is a luggage designer, manufacturer, and retailer, and similar to Glossier, is direct-to-consumer with a handful of brick-and-mortar stores. The idea came after Rubio broke a suitcase and reached out to a bunch of well-traveled friends as to where she should find a replacement. No one had anywhere compelling to recommend, so Stephanie and Jennifer turned their thinking to creating a luggage brand, using what they knew from their Warby Parker days to get going.

Stephanie and Jennifer had to pivot right out of the gate with Away. They had hoped to have their first round of luggage available for Christmas but as the deadline approached, they realized their first production run wouldn't be ready in time. Instead of being able to offer luggage, they harnessed the power of influencers and creatives (writers, artists, and photographers) to build a community who'd be happy to share more about the luggage when it arrived. The duo decided to create a beautiful hardcover book called *The Places We Return To*, featuring these contributors. They sold the book in November 2015, along with a gift card that was redeemable for a suitcase, essentially creating a preorder strategy for the luggage.

The pair's ingenuity was rewarded with the contributors sharing generously and mentioning the impending launch of the luggage, which gave them a solid platform from which to start the brand. The company's first-year sales clocked in at over $12 million, an amazing feat for any start-up. Fast forward this success story to today and you'll discover that Away has sold over one million suitcases, raised $151 million to aid in its growth, and also secured its spot in the unicorn club with a valuation of $1.4 billion.

> ## Don't find customers for your products, find products for your customers.
> ### SETH GODIN

At the start of Business Chicks, I had a bunch of relationships and a reasonably good-sized database through my recruitment company that I could tap into. I knew I was giving myself the best possible shot at success, because I had a ready-made group of potential customers. It meant that I could easily (well, quite easily) get over 500 people to my first event. Trying to get it off the ground with just my mom and her friends wouldn't have had anywhere near the same result.

At the end of the day, almost everything in business comes back to sales. You can have the best idea in the world, but without a solid distribution strategy and a strong path to sales, you're just another candle business.

THEY QUIT THEIR DAY JOBS TOO SOON. If you have aspirations of starting a business, you don't always have to leave one form of income behind altogether. Alyce Tran's luxury accessories empire The Daily Edited started out as a style blog. Alyce and her cofounder, Tania Liu, admit that they didn't think anyone would look at the blog initially, so they tried turning it into a clothing collection, but that failed after eighteen months. It was only when Alyce struggled to find a clutch that was reasonably priced but didn't look cheap that they made the move into monogrammed accessories, selling direct to the audience they'd accidentally built on social media. Their initial $7,000 worth of product sold out in just three days, and over the next few years, Alyce and Tania continued to work their day jobs while building their business on the side.

It wasn't until Alyce sat down with her accountant that she finally decided to throw in the towel on her paid gig and go full-time with The Daily Edited. "My accountant told me that we were doing over $200,000 a month and it was clear we were growing significantly. He said, 'You realize you're selling a lot of stuff. You could quit your day job and work on this if you really want to. It could be something.'" Alyce says about that time, "I didn't realize! I was just doing it all, just trying to get through everything, not knowing where I was going." Today, The Daily Edited has an annual turnover of more than $30 million and has expanded into the US and Singapore.

When I first bought Business Chicks, there was a period where I was trying to do two jobs. I would get to the office and start my "normal job" with my recruitment agency at 7:30 a.m. I'd work until about 7:00 p.m., then I'd go back to my tiny little apartment, which was about a five-minute walk from the office, to start working on Business Chicks. I'd sit on the floor, processing the booking forms that had been faxed in that day for an upcoming event and entering them into a spreadsheet. I'd process the raffle ticket sales. I'd send requests to prospective guest speakers. And I'd pitch to brands that I wanted to partner with.

I'd do whatever it took and work whatever hours were needed to get it off the ground and turn it into something. It wasn't until Business

Chicks was starting to hum and I could see massive potential that I decided to exit the recruitment company and make it my new day job.

THEY OVERPLAN AND FAIL TO PIVOT. While it's brilliant to have a game plan and a big-picture vision, you also need to remain flexible as to how things could turn out. I'm always a little skeptical when I hear that companies have five-year or ten-year plans. It's great to have a concept of how you'd like things to go, but business moves at such a pace these days that it's often difficult to plan out much further than one or two years.

Netflix began as a DVD distribution service, with cofounder Marc Randolph getting his start by sending DVDs in the mail to customers. It's now the world's leading Internet television network, with over 140 million members in more than 190 countries enjoying more than 125 million hours of TV shows and movies each day. You couldn't imagine a more different model and business to the one Randolph founded. What mattered was that he started somewhere and wasn't fixated on the outcome.

Compare this agility with the Blockbuster video brand, whose brick-and-mortar offering remained flat-footed in the face of innovations such as Netflix. It's a perfect example of not pivoting quickly enough and, therefore, being left behind.

THEY USE CAPITAL RAISING AS AN EXCUSE TO NOT START. I've built my businesses without any external investment, but I've never been short on offers. I'm not going to lie—sometimes these offers are tempting. But with any investment from a third party, there's new pressure. Suddenly, you have to answer their questions and spend lots of time reporting on results. Keeping your investors up to date can be really distracting from actually building your business, and it's at that stage that winging it in other areas of your business becomes that much harder.

For the most part, outside investors are looking for high growth and a quick exit, or a very clear path to a successful exit. They're seeking a return on their money and want growth at all costs.

One option for anyone looking at the investor route is to build a business so attractive that, eventually, people will throw money at you to get in on the action, rather than the other way around. It's not always the best idea to get fixated on raising money. It can often distract you from starting and building a fantastic business. Once you have a strong business that churns out cash and has a great reputation, investors will come knocking.

> ## Great companies start because the founders want to change the world ... not make a fast buck.
> ### GUY KAWASAKI

Carly de Castro is cofounder of Pressed Juicery, which she founded with two partners back in 2010 after she dramatically changed her lifestyle and began to see the health benefits of cold-pressed juicing. Turning her passion into a business, Carly and her partners launched their first outlet, a tiny 22-square-foot shopfront in Brentwood, California, wondering whether they'd make enough sales in the first week to pay the staff they'd hired. Turns out they did, and since then, the concept has taken off with over sixty retail locations in California, Hawaii, Nevada, Washington, and New York. Carly and her partners self-funded for the first six years because they wanted to keep integrity with the products and the brand. When they eventually did take on external capital, it was with a small family fund that continued to allow them control, but also to keep growing.

THEY FORGET THE BASICS. This may sound like 101 because it is: you need to make more money than you spend. Business is actually that simple. Serious cash flow issues only arise if your business isn't making enough money and your expenses are more than you earn.

THEY WAIT UNTIL THEY HAVE ALL THE MONEY IN THE BANK. I've always favored bootstrapping as a way to get a company off the ground, because it can show pretty quickly whether you've got a viable business model or not. Bootstrapping means starting a business with very little money and relying on customer funds to fuel growth, just like Pressed Juicery did. Entrepreneurs of bootstrapped companies have to figure out how to attract paying customers if they're to survive. You usually find that people who have bootstrapped are the most resilient and war-wounded entrepreneurs—they've had to wing it every day in order to work out how to make payroll, pay the bills, and still fund growth.

Bootstrapping is not for the fainthearted. This type of funding requires discipline and stamina. Founders risk everything by putting in sweat equity and hoping it pays off. Bootstrapping entrepreneurs have to learn to build great partnerships, inspire people with their vision, barter when they don't have cash, and above all, hustle hard. Desperation often breeds creativity.

Most entrepreneurs who bootstrap their companies have an "I'm in it for the long haul" mindset. They quietly and slowly chip away at building a quality business over time. Bootstrapping means you answer to no one else, which allows you to give 100 percent of your focus to trying to make it work. It also means you have to continually innovate if you're to survive, getting creative with ways to make money.

It does have a bunch of downsides, of course. Bootstrapped companies never seem to have enough money, and growth can be a lot slower.

THEY TRY TO DO TOO MUCH. A lot of people start out with too broad an offering, throwing too many ideas, products, or services up against a wall and hoping that one of them sticks.

You're a lifestyle brand that sells clothes, homewares, fragrances, candles, and accessories. Or a creative who can build websites, generate an ad campaign, write copy, design business cards, redo packaging, and redesign a logo while you're at it. The problem I see happening time and time again is that these people take on too much too quickly and spread themselves too thin. Also, when you're not known as a brand you need to keep it simple for people to refer customers your way. If people aren't 100 percent clear about what you do, they're going to be less enthusiastic to recommend people to you. I call it the Grandfather Test. Your elderly grandfather should be able to clearly understand what you do from your description because you've simplified it so much that it's easy for everyone to articulate.

My advice would be to go an inch wide and a mile deep: try one idea, product, or service to begin with, and do it really well. A lot of iconic brands—Coca-Cola, Duracell, Spanx—all started out selling just one thing.

The McDonald brothers started out just making hamburgers and fries. Microsoft started with a computer. Amazon started as a marketplace for books. Business Chicks is now a multimedia business, but when we first started out, we just did events—and we did them better than anyone else.

Los Angeles hairstylist Alli Webb started a mobile blow wave service from the back of her car. Eleven years on, she now owns more than one hundred salons across the US and Canada under her Drybar brand. While the scale of Alli's business has grown exponentially over the years, her services have not. The business offers blowouts and nothing else.

"We've felt very strongly about focusing on one thing and being really great at it," Alli says. "Although I understand we're all so busy that it'd be nice while you're having your hair done [to also have] someone . . . do your nails, I think that it would convolute the brand too much if we tried to do other things."

There's time in the future to become a successful multiproduct company (if that's your wish). If you're starting out, though, focus on winning the game you're in before expanding into other product areas.

THEY LOSE FOCUS. When I look back on my many failures, they all come back to one thing: a lack of focus. There have been times when I've tried too many things at once, or dropped the ball by abdicating too much responsibility to others when my full focus and attention were needed.

When we moved into our first real office, we had to rent the entire space and, therefore, had two floors to work with. We only needed one floor at the time to accommodate our small team, so I thought the best thing would be to open another business on the extra floor.

At the time, I was a fitness junkie, training with a personal trainer five mornings a week, running in my spare time, and trying any new workout fad that came along. I'd recently discovered these cool new vacuum and compression machines and had become instantly hooked. The company who manufactured the machines was offering franchises, so I thought, "I'll give this a shot," and I bought one. Within a matter of weeks, we had set up the studio and hired some staff, and the customers started trickling in.

Looking back, I knew deep down we were never going to set the world on fire with that business. Initially, it was sort of enough for me that we were able to utilize a redundant space and that I'd get to use the fitness equipment I'd bought from time to time. As the weeks passed, I realized that it was going to need a lot more of my time if it were to become a success. The reality of running the business set in. Day in and day out, it would be the same. Not many surprises. Just a grind.

I'm much better in a business where there are lots of moving parts and lots of variety—it's not knowing what's coming next every day that keeps me interested.

I could have become motivated and worked out how to market the concept well and get loads more customers through the doors, but the truth is, I just wasn't passionate about it. Every day, I'd walk up the stairs past the fitness studio and find myself not even wanting to go in there, so, inevitably, the time came when I had to have a tough conversation with myself. Here's what me, myself, and I talked about:

- The funds I'd sunk into the venture would have been better invested in the business I was already in and was already passionate about.
- The fitness business was a distraction and draining my energy. To make any business work, you need all the energy you can muster.

- It didn't matter that I'd spent a lot up until that point. Better to cut my losses and move on.

So that's what I did. I sold the equipment, closed the doors (well, opened them up and created a big meeting space for our team), and moved on. I didn't allow myself time to wallow or get upset—that would have just been another waste of my energy.

The lesson for me was that if your business is to succeed, it requires two things: your passion and your focus. If you can't find either of those, then maybe it's time to call it quits.

THEY FOCUS ON THE WRONG THINGS. If you're starting out, don't worry about your logo, your business card, or your stationery. You've got time for that later. Right now, just go do the things that will actually start building your business. Learn to avoid the tempting "busy stuff" that makes you feel like you're getting ahead. Go get a meaty, paying client. Do good work. Bill for it. Don't rush to the urgent at the expense of the important.

Also, unless you're creating a brand that uses social media as a strong sales channel, don't waste time having an unnecessary focus there. And if you really can't help yourself, just pick one platform and do it well. At a Business Chicks event in 2013, Zoë Foster Blake, founder of Go-To Skin Care, agreed, saying, "There are too many digital mouths to feed. Pick one or two platforms and do them really well."

THEY SPEND TOO MUCH ON THE WRONG THINGS. When it comes to marketing and publicity, I've always favored the approach of pretending you have no budget to begin with. The thing about working to no budget is that it forces you to get inventive and work out how you can create value from a baseline of nothing. The alternative is putting aside a budget to spend, say, $100,000, in which case, you get into a dangerous habit of trying to solve the problem of "Okay, how do I divvy it up and spend this money?" instead of being frugal and valuing every dollar you spend. Budgets, while often necessary, breed laziness in most people.

When Lizzy Abegg and her sister Isabella Pennefather first launched the Byron Bay fashion label Spell & The Gypsy Collective, they sold exclusively at the local markets.

Ten years later, the label is such a runaway success that its modern bohemian designs have been worn by the likes of Blake Lively, Sienna Miller, and Kate Hudson. New items have been known to sell out within a few hours (sometimes minutes!) of being listed on the brand's website.

Despite their size and success, until recently, Lizzy and Isabella had never invested a cent in traditional marketing.

Instead of relying on conventional tactics such as print advertising and direct mail to grow their audience, Lizzy says you simply need to know where your people are and build a community around your brand. For Spell, this has largely been Instagram, and it's here that the Spell team lovingly curates content and messaging that inspires their tribe, complemented by a beautiful website and storytelling.

"We have grown our social media community organically by being authentic and openly sharing our lives through the stories we share on social media," Lizzy said to me. "Our vision has always been to inspire beautifully, so our approach has been to create and share content that shows a glimpse of that magic we make and see every day. I've seen so many new brands begin with what is clearly a very structured, premeditated branding strategy; their website is polished and their brand guidelines are watertight—which is exactly the opposite of how it's been for us. We were trading at the markets and online before we even had a logo, and it wasn't until seven years into our business we even considered creating brand guidelines."

What the Spell philosophy shows is that you don't need to have huge marketing budgets to get the word out. What you really need is a story to tell, a market to tell it to, and the ability to do it creatively each time.

THEY'RE LED BY WHAT THEIR CUSTOMERS THINK THEY WANT.
Henry Ford is contentiously credited as saying that if he'd asked his

customers what they wanted, they would have said faster horses. Most customers don't actually know what they want until you put it in front of them. While it's important to listen and accept feedback, if you spend too much time trying to bend to what they think they want, you'll lose sight of who you really are.

Lizzy Abegg says it's important that your product comes from a place of authenticity. She says that as Spell & The Gypsy Collective has grown, the ideas from customers about what they should create can be overwhelming and she has to say to her designer sister, Isabella, "Just sketch something really *you*."

THEY DON'T TIME THEIR GROWTH RIGHT. The biggest expense in any small business is going to be the people you hire. You want to make sure that you maximize your investment, and their talents, from the moment they walk in your door.

If you don't have a clear path for how they're going to return their salary (plus employment costs) and then some, maybe think about whether the timing of the hire is right. Over the years, we've developed organizational capabilities in certain areas of the business, such as our in-house events team. We're constantly analyzing this team's workload to see if they're at capacity or not. If they've got room to move, then we try to get a little busier with a new event product. In the same way airlines want their planes to be in the sky earning them money and not staying grounded, you want your people to be working at or near their capacity. If you can't find them work or projects to do, it's going to be difficult to grow (and you may find yourself going backward). It's a fine line.

THEY'RE TOO PICKY. Fashion illustrator Megan Hess says she took every single job that came her way in the early days. She started out designing pizza boxes, and once completed a 350-page horse care manual only to find out the project wasn't going ahead. One night, Megan received a call from a New York publisher telling her that Candace Bushnell wanted her to illustrate all of her book covers, including *Sex and the City*. "That was the moment everything changed for me," says Megan, who has gone on to illustrate for Chanel, Dior, Tiffany & Co., and Louis Vuitton.

If you're waiting for your perfect client, you may be waiting for a while. Do the work that pays until you can say no to the jobs that don't excite you and a big fat yes to the ones that do.

THEY FORGET WHY THEY STARTED. When your why is clear, your how becomes easy. When you know why you're building a business, figuring out solutions to the problems you face is really easy. If you're not sure why, then it can all feel like one big drag.

THEIR PARTNERSHIPS FAIL. When deciding if you need a business partner, give a lot of consideration to who you go into business with. Don't do it just because it's convenient or you think it might be a good idea, or because you have no other options. If you're sure you've found the perfect partner, you should still future-proof yourself from dramas that may arise by getting a watertight shareholder's agreement and doing a ton of detailed scenario planning so both parties are clear from the outset.

THEY THINK TOO SMALL. I'm here to tell you that it's much easier to run a big business than it is to run a small business. When your business gets to a certain size, you have access to resources and people who can free you up to do whatever it is you want to do. The stress doesn't go away, but the reliance on you does. I see a lot of people starting businesses with the intention of remaining small. I ask them about where they see their companies in five years' time, and they say, "Oh, it'll just be a boutique PR agency. In five years' time, we'll have ten staff and have bought our own small office." Why limit yourself with the language of "just" and "boutique"? Why not start out by imagining buying the whole floor of an office building instead of a single office suite? Of course, this is completely acceptable if it is truly what's in your heart and the vision you have for yourself, but don't let the default position be thinking small.

THEY DON'T GET OUT MUCH. Lots of people spend too much time in their businesses. They aren't taking the time to meet others, learn more, enjoy themselves, and treat their teams. So, here's the shameless plug.

You should join Business Chicks, not just because we're the nicest bunch of people on the planet, but because networking matters, and some of that inspiration is bound to rub off on you.

CHERISH YOUR CUSTOMERS

On the day Rowan and I got engaged, he booked us into a suite at a hotel in the city. As we were checking in, I excitedly told the manager behind the counter that we had just gotten engaged. He looked up for a moment, congratulated us, and then said, "Sorry, your room isn't ready yet."

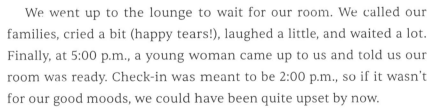

Every great business is built on friendship.

JC PENNEY

We went up to the lounge to wait for our room. We called our families, cried a bit (happy tears!), laughed a little, and waited a lot. Finally, at 5:00 p.m., a young woman came up to us and told us our room was ready. Check-in was meant to be 2:00 p.m., so if it wasn't for our good moods, we could have been quite upset by now.

We were positive there'd be some consolation for having to wait three hours for our room, but when we got to our suite there was nothing. No "sorry we kept you waiting." No "congratulations on your engagement." Not even a free bottle of water.

Flash forward to our ten-year wedding anniversary and the experience couldn't have been more different. *This* hotel didn't skip a beat arranging room upgrades, a personalized souvenir with our photo on it, our favorite cocktails, tickets out on their catamaran, an amazing celebratory cake, and the list goes on. Given we're a party of eight these days, perhaps we're just more attractive customers now? Whatever the reason, you can quickly see which hotel I'll be returning to and recommending to my friends.

The key to superb customer service is always how you make people feel. You have to make them feel something. There are a million ways to do this, but one of the easiest is to up the ante when there's a lot of emotion involved, because that's when a customer's experience of your brand is heightened.

Think of how you felt when you got engaged or married, celebrated a major birthday, had a baby, or sold a family home. If a company can learn to harness this emotional energy for the better, they can turn a customer into their most loyal of fans.

If you're a real estate agent, that might mean placing a welcome basket on the kitchen counter for each new home buyer for the day they move in. If you sell cars, you might find out the customer's favorite song and have it playing when they pick up the car or place a bunch of flowers on the front passenger seat. And if you're in the hospitality game and you mess up the check-in of a newly engaged couple, just give them a bottle of cheap champagne already.

Give them something to talk about

When I first set up Business Chicks, we had no money, but we did have a lot of love to give, so we started there. Loving our customers hard led to them talking about us. That then led to their friends becoming customers, and so the cycle continued. And we all know it's more affordable to keep an existing customer than it is to always be on the hunt for new ones.

Brands that value good customer service don't miss a trick. They know that to impress a customer, they're going to have to bring their A game and do something so meaningful that it becomes significant enough to be talked about.

Zappos is the perfect example of this. Zappos founder Tony Hsieh has always maintained that even though they primarily started out selling shoes, the company doesn't consider itself a shoe company. Instead, it considers itself a customer service company and will do whatever it takes to make you feel like you matter.

There's one particular story I love from the playbook of Zappos's amazing customer service. Back in 2007, a woman named Zaz Lamarr missed the deadline to return some shoes after her mom passed away. When Zappos called to ask about the shoes, Zaz told them what had happened. Zappos immediately sent a courier to pick up the shoes (which was, of course, not a standard company practice), and it also sent Zaz a bouquet of flowers, acknowledging the loss of her mom.

Zaz later wrote about the experience online saying: "When I came home from town, a florist delivery man was just leaving. It was a beautiful arrangement in a basket with white lilies and roses and carnations. Big and lush and fragrant. I opened the card, and it was from Zappos. I burst into tears. I'm a sucker for kindness, and if that isn't one of the nicest things I've ever had happen to me, I don't know what is."

Not your typical shoe company, right?

Great brands know that the key to strong customer service is to prioritize the person before the task. It's all about connecting with your customer, making them feel wanted and valued, and then working out what they need from you.

If you focus on your customer instead of shelling out tens of thousands of dollars on the world's best logo, stationery, advertising campaign, and brochures, you may just be in with a shot. When you build a business worth talking about, lots of the work will be done for you.

Here are the essentials that make good brands great and get them noticed.

THEY TAKE THEIR TIME. When our customers arrive at our events and come to registration to collect their name badges, we try to encourage our front-facing event crew to welcome them first. We tell them that it's not about picking up a name badge, it's about making a friend. We inspire them to connect first, and then serve. Connecting might mean a "Hi, welcome, and thanks for coming along! Did you find us okay?" or "Hi, I'm Michelle, it's so great to have you here with us." The final step is helping the customer to find their name badge and getting them registered. Customer first, task second.

Too many people are quick to get to the task with a "How can I help you today?" cutting the customer off and making them feel rushed. Unless you're working at McDonald's, trying to serve your customers in sixty seconds or less, there's no need to hurry them out of your way. Customers are not an interruption—they're the reason your business exists.

No matter how busy you are, you should never give off the air of being too busy. Take a breath, get present, put a smile on your dial, and be there for others, no matter what's going on behind the scenes. I've trained myself to do this over the years. There are always one million thoughts racing through my head at our events, but it's my job to be completely calm, like a swan—peaceful and in full control above the water, but below the surface, the legs are moving at a rapid pace.

Make a customer, not a sale.
KATHERINE BARCHETTI

Quick tip: if you're hiring for a position where the person is going to have to speak to customers on the phone, be sure to speak with the candidate at length on the phone before you hire them. Did they make you feel good? Were they inherently happy and upbeat? Could they express themselves well? Did you feel that they could strike a good balance between getting the job done efficiently and leaving the customer feeling uplifted and taken care of?

THEIR CUSTOMERS KNOW WHAT TO EXPECT. In the same way that your job as a manager is to remove frustrations for your people, your job in serving your customers is to remove confusion for them. Your customers should always know where they stand. They should know which way to go. They should know what's coming up next. They should be left without any confusion of what they're going to be given and what to expect.

THEY BREAK THE RULES FROM TIME TO TIME. The grocery market is highly competitive in America, and it takes a special brand to distinguish itself. One Christmas Day, an elderly gentleman in Pennsylvania was snowed in with no way of getting groceries. His daughter had called around to several retailers, but none of them could help. She eventually told her story to grocery store Trader Joe's, who jumped on it. Even though Trader Joe's didn't offer a delivery service, they sent a staff member to the eighty-nine-year-old's home and delivered the fifty dollar order his daughter had placed. And the best bit was that they didn't charge her a cent. They wished him "Happy holidays," and the story had a happy ending, with Trader Joe's becoming a hero on social media over the days that followed.

As leaders, it's about giving your team permission to do whatever they can to make someone's day. My team knows that if it's going to make a customer happy, they have carte blanche to do what feels right to them. It's part of the culture that we've built, and nothing makes me happier than when a member tells me something that one of my team has done and I've had no idea about it. Mission accomplished.

THEY SEE CUSTOMER SERVICE AS EVERYONE'S JOB. Like anything, customer service comes from the top. If, as a leader, you're not willing to actively engage with customers, why would the rest of your team be? I'm acutely aware that it's my job to lead this, and I always make an effort to speak with our members as much as I can.

Quick tip: if you're on the phone and responsible for taking customer phone calls, always keep a pen and paper handy next to you, so that the second they say their name, you can jot it down and use it throughout the conversation. Also, smile while you're on the phone—it works!

THEY RESPOND—AND QUICKLY. The secret to getting customer service right is balancing how quick and efficient you can be without making the customer feel dismissed. These rules apply online too, where customers' demands are higher than ever before. More and more consumers are using social media to communicate with brands, and we expect our questions to be met with a quick reply.

One survey found that social media users expect an answer to feedback within four hours of sending a message, but it typically takes brands an average of ten hours to respond—and that's if they respond at all. That same survey found that brands respond to just 11 percent of the messages they receive.

THEY PRESENT THEMSELVES WELL. It goes without saying that if you're in a front-facing customer service role, how you present yourself is critical. If you can't take the time to care enough about how you present yourself, how will you ever be able to show you care about another person?

THEY GO ABOVE AND BEYOND TO MAKE THEIR CUSTOMERS FEEL SOMETHING. If you have the opportunity to give a sensory experience, appealing to the customer's five senses, then do it. I'm lucky to travel a lot with my work and I've stayed in some of the world's best hotels. The ones that have blown me away are those that have thought about what you see, hear, touch, taste, and smell the moment you enter your room: the lighting is perfect, there's music playing subtly in the background, there are different textures for you to run your hands over (perhaps the smooth sheets on the bed or the back of a textured armchair), they leave some fresh fruit or chocolates out to welcome you, and it smells fresh and clean. Even if you can't do all five, try doing as many as you can. Even just turning on music in the background can make a huge difference in how a person experiences your brand.

Stores are the same. A great retail experience will appeal to all the senses, and the brands that get it right pay attention to how bright the lighting is (bye-bye, fluorescence), and they invest in fresh flowers or burn candles and give you lots of things to touch and feel. A number of retailers even have time-sensitive lighting in the changing rooms now. You press "evening" to see how the outfit you're trying on will look at night, or "daytime" for how it will be seen in brighter light.

Virgin America is the only airline I know that has music playing when customers are checking in. It's genius, because the check-in experience at airports can be stressful, and their music goes a long way toward setting the scene and making you feel relaxed.

If you're lucky enough to be an employer, also remember that your people are your customers too. Treat them just as you would your paying customers—serve them, surprise them, support them, and go above and beyond.

THE TURNING POINT

Stepping back to drive a business forward

Entrepreneurs are brave and unusual creatures. We create, we innovate, we push boundaries, we challenge our people to be more, we take risks, and we dream. In my case, though, that's about all I can do. I'm not a great manager of people and problems. I prefer to spend my time dreaming up the next idea and then getting everyone into action to make it happen. That's pretty easy to do when you have a small team of thirty people or fewer. You have relationships with everyone in the business, and communication is quick and nimble. Ironing out problems at that size is relatively easy, and getting things done is usually fun rather than hard. The problems can come when your business needs to expand beyond your own capacity.

Admitting that the business you started and lovingly grew for years needs someone else's management is a big deal. When I first bought Business Chicks, I did everything. It's safe to say that there's not a task in my business that I haven't done, and I'm proud of that. It also gives me tremendous insight into what's possible and how long things should take. We've come a long way since those days. As the business grew larger, I felt that a new skill set was required and more rigorous management needed to be put in place. And at some point, about ten years in, I had to come to terms with the fact that the person to do all that wasn't me.

The turning point manifested in two situations, within a week of each other. The first time I sensed it was the night after launching Business Chicks in America. We started off with a huge bang by presenting Arianna Huffington in Los Angeles, and that evening, I was invited to her home for a meal. Not one to turn down impulsive, last-minute invitations, my colleague Bec came with me, and we took ourselves off to Arianna's house.

We sat outside in the garden of her beautiful home, enjoying an amazing Greek feast. Afterward, on the way back to our hotel, I turned to Bec and said, "We're going to do this. I can't believe we're actually going to do this. We're going to take this thing global and we're going to do it really well." Of course, at that point I had no idea how, but I knew it could be possible. "We just need good people," I told Bec enthusiastically, and I'm not sure whether it was she or I who suggested it, but I whipped out my phone straightaway. I texted Amber Kingsley.

Amber interned for me at Business Chicks back when it was just the two of us at a desk we'd built ourselves in my first tiny office. She quickly became the first Business Chicks employee on the payroll and was instrumental in initially setting up the business with me. She had since moved home to New Zealand. Every day I missed having her by my side, and I felt her steadiness was what was needed to get to the next level, so I asked her to come back. Within minutes she'd texted back with her reply: "Okay, sure!"

The next insight that brought me closer to knowing I needed someone in the business to replace me was spending time with Jane Wurwand. Jane cofounded skincare brand Dermalogica, and I basically want to be her when I grow up. Jane is one of the most intelligent and thoughtful businesswomen on the planet and conducts herself with the highest level of integrity and grace wherever she goes.

When I first met Jane (she was our guest speaker in San Francisco) it was like meeting a kindred spirit. Over a few years now, I've come to value her counsel and insights enormously. Thinking seriously about appointing a CEO to my company, I consulted with Jane about her experiences. She told me that, in hindsight, there were times she wished she'd recruited her CEOs from within the business rather than externally. Jane said it was a bonus to hire internally as the person would know the company's DNA inside out, and they would've been working intimately with you for a long time, too, so they would know how the founder's mind works.

Olivia Ruello and I had worked together on and off for the better part of ten years by that point. When I thought about who could conceivably be up for the challenge, I knew it was her. I trusted her. She knew how I worked. And I also liked that she'd been out of my companies for a little bit of time and had earned some stripes elsewhere. We started talking, and before I knew it, I had Amber back in the general manager role and Olivia seriously considering the chief executive role.

In a lot of ways, handing over the reins of your company is a beautiful surrendering, but it also comes with a case of the I-wasn't-good-enoughs. Whenever I started feeling this way, I kept coming back to the fact that I'm an entrepreneur, a dreamer, and a visionary, and these are all good things if channeled well. There was someone much better out there to take my business to the next level, and by turning things over to them, I freed myself up to concentrate on the big picture, which is where I belonged.

Take charge and don't apologize for it

There's a fine line between stepping away from your business and making sure you retain enough control to guarantee the company stays on course.

Fashion brand Nasty Gal's founder Sophia Amoruso learned this lesson the hard way. Sophia's rise to success is such a compelling story that it was made into a Netflix original series, *Girlboss*. Sophia made her start by selling vintage clothes on eBay, and this soon turned into a much bigger venture, eventually spinning off into brick-and-mortar retail too. At the age of twenty-eight, Sophia was running a $100 million business and had carved out a following as a young entrepreneur to watch, being featured as one of "America's richest women under thirty" on the cover of *Forbes* magazine and receiving various other accolades.

> **I'm the one who decides, but I like having lots of other people with whom I can discuss ideas.**
> **GIORGIO ARMANI**

While she'd never been interested in accepting venture capital into her business, the news of her success started spreading and the phones ran hot with offers from investors. These investors promised much faster growth than she could achieve on her own. They promised larger warehouses, a more skilled executive team, better offices, and more. Sophia eventually took on an equity partner, and the growth that the investors had promised was actualized. But not too long after, it all headed south.

Sophia was in Australia for a series of appearances with Business Chicks around the time of her company's demise. I was touring with her, and our first event was in Brisbane. At that event, Sophia was candid, upbeat, funny, and wise, and lived up to her reputation of being a no-holds-barred, say-what-you-think young woman. The next day in Melbourne, though, her mood was different. The normally effervescent Sophia was more considered and maybe even a little glum. I couldn't put my finger on what it was and dismissed it as jetlag. Afterward, as my team and I were clearing security at the airport on our way to our next event in Sydney, I received a distressed phone call from one of my event managers. "Em, this hasn't hit the Australian news yet, but it's just broken in the US. Nasty Gal has just filed for bankruptcy."

The timing couldn't have been worse. We were due to take the stage in front of almost 2,000 women the next morning. A quick Google search showed that the news had most definitely been broadcast over US media already, although the presidential election was also in full swing that week, so it possibly didn't get as much airtime as it normally might have.

The next morning, before we went onstage, I spent a lot of time with Sophia in the green room, trying to make her feel comfortable. We talked about how we'd have to address the bankruptcy in our interview together, and I promised I'd approach it as gently as possible and with the utmost respect. She agreed, knowing it was the only option we had. I was so proud of her for even turning up that morning, let alone handling herself so beautifully. Onstage, she was vulnerable and real, shedding a few tears when we got to the part about her business going bankrupt. "You guys, it was my first business, and I got really, really far!" she said as the tears flowed.

Sophia was unequivocally certain about what had led to the company's demise: it was because she'd abdicated too much responsibility. Because Nasty Gal had gotten so big so quickly, it had spiraled out of control. Sophia had placed too much blind faith in her leadership team and in her investors. She admitted that she should have stayed closer and demanded she control the decision-making. Her subsequent advice was, "women need to be controlling their businesses." If you have a company that is so deeply tied to the founder, you can't escape the strong DNA of that person, and you can't underestimate the impact of their absence, either.

I've watched this play out with several of my friends and their businesses. They get to a certain size and start to corporatize the company, and before they know it, they're making far less money and experiencing more headaches. There's a big difference between running a good-sized nimble business that can still make decisions quickly and not lose itself in bureaucracy, and running one that gets so big so fast that it dilutes its success with unnecessary processes and ego-driven leadership (from others, not you).

Sophia has gone on to use this experience to fuel the creation of her new business—a media company called, you guessed it, *Girlboss*. You go, girl.

"It's failure that gives you the
proper perspective on success."

ELLEN DEGENERES

Whichever path you choose, choose great people and great leadership, but above all, choose to stay in control.

FAIL SPECTACULARLY

Sir James Dyson went through 5,126 failed prototypes to develop his vacuum cleaner; the 5,127th worked. Arianna Huffington's second book, *After Reason*, was knocked back by thirty-six publishers. And Steven Spielberg was rejected by the University of Southern California School of Cinematic Arts three times. Failure hurts, but it's not permanent.

I failed spectacularly at making Business Chicks in the US a success on my first attempt. I hated every single moment of it. While I'd had smaller business failures, none had hurt anywhere near as deeply as this one.

For the first six months of living in the States, I was racked with stress. There were precious few days that I woke up without a mouthful of canker sores or, even worse, a cold sore. Headaches were a given, and feeling so overwhelmed that I could just break into tears at any given moment was the new norm.

I had seriously underestimated how much it would impact me to be away from my local team, to not have the support I was used to, and to not be able to just call my mom on the way home from work without calculating the time difference. Close relationships were my lifeline back home. I had rarely experienced stress or felt overwhelmed, because I had so many people around me to help out whenever I needed it. My team would just say to me, "Okay, Isaacs, what's up?" as if they could read my mind. But in the US, with no one around and the kids needing more of me, and Rowan figuring out what he was going to do for work, it's fair to say I felt very alone.

At first, all was fine, as is often the case. By the time we made the move from Australia, my team had produced about twenty events across San Francisco, Los Angeles, and New York, and we'd started to get some good traction. We had an office up and running in New York and a team working from there for almost a year. Even though they were there, I'd decided to base myself on the west coast in Los Angeles, as the lifestyle was more suitable for our big family, the flight back home was easier, and the time difference was a little kinder too.

On the day after we arrived, I flung myself into action (what jetlag?), getting my events team to agree on a date and book a venue at a snazzy Beverly Hills hotel for an event. I asked my friends Lorna Jane Clarkson, founder of Lorna Jane, and Jane Wurwand to speak, and they kindly agreed. We came up with a name for the event, hustled hard to sell it out, and we did. The problem was that we made approximately $1,000, which was not even enough to cover the airfares of my team coming in from New York City.

Over the course of the next twelve or so months, we signed up over 4,000 new members and held another dozen events. The problem wasn't the interest in our brand. People loved everything we stood for and kept wanting more. The feedback was exactly what we wanted to hear: "There's nothing like Business Chicks!" "I'm telling all my friends!" "When's your next get-together?" At one evening event in New York City, there was a group of four women lingering afterward. After I said my goodbyes and was about halfway out of the room, they yelled out in unison, "Business Chicks rocks!" at the top of their voices. I smiled all the way home, thinking about how these strangers could possibly love something that I'd created on the other side of the world ten years prior.

I knew what we had was special and unique, and I knew that people wanted it. We were filling ballrooms with 700 guests for our large-scale events with no problems, but it's just so darn expensive to produce an event in the US. There are hidden taxes and costs at every turn, and the end result was that we'd lose a bunch of money each time.

Month after month, the US business was bleeding the healthy Australian business dry of cash. Row and I were paying a 10 percent mortgage rate on the home we'd just bought because, being so new to the country, we had no credit rating. The salaries, taxes, health insurance, and office rent in the US were exorbitant, and we just could not stop hemorrhaging money. We'd already immersed ourselves in a crash course working out the complex US taxation system through a lot of expensive advice, and everywhere we turned, it felt like we were facing another bill, with precious little revenue trickling in to alleviate the pain.

I remember the day it all kind of hit home. I'd asked my assistant to head out and buy some things for my son Ryder's first birthday party. She came back with a bunch of items on the list but said that the card didn't go through when she'd tried at the last store. After buying a house and getting ourselves set up to this point, we'd run clean out of all the money I'd put aside to fund our move. And we really had no way to make more.

I found myself in a funny predicament. Everything looked shiny from the outside, and in many ways it was. We had already built a following; we had paying customers and members wanting more. Behind the scenes, though, I was confused and stuck, not knowing which way to turn. People would ask, "How's the US going?" on my trips back to Australia, and I hadn't even formed my thoughts enough to know exactly what to say.

Eventually, we had to let some team members go, which was awful. I avoided it for a good couple of months, but that only added to the problem. When I had to make the call, it was like a dagger to the heart, for me and for them. These people had been very loyal, believing in my vision and working to the best of their abilities. It wasn't their fault that we were underfunded and everything cost a bomb, but I faced the decision of either semi-closing the US business and taking a breather, or having my healthy business in Australia go under through trying.

In the middle of the ordeal, I confided in Sir Richard Branson and told him how I was well and truly on my way to failing hard. He was comforting and helped put it all in perspective for me, mentioning a bunch of his business disasters, such as Virgin Cars and another few I'd never heard of before.

> There will come a time when you believe
> everything is finished. That will
> just be the beginning.
>
> **LOUIS L'AMOUR**

We all know Richard is forever trying to be the challenger brand and shake up industries. There's an ongoing joke that if you've never heard of half of his businesses, it's probably because they weren't worth knowing about. In 1994, he launched Virgin Cola to rival Coca-Cola, and a few years later he took on the wedding industry with Virgin Brides. He's had countless other failures too—Virgin Clothing, Virgin Pulse, Virgin Lottery—but when you talk to him, you learn that he's totally down with all of them. In his mind, failure is just another factor of business you'd better get good at. It's also comforting to know that lots of Silicon Valley investors won't even consider funding an entrepreneur who hasn't lived through at least one failed venture.

What I learned and what surprised me a little about this whole experience is that it didn't hurt to lose the money. I mean, it was a total pain in the ass and we had to solve the problem and it kept me up at night, but it has just never solely been about the money for me. I'd happily have no money if I could still live out a life of playing big and having a go.

Fail fast. Recover faster.

Over the years, we've received a fair amount of resistance to the name "Business Chicks." The people who know the brand love it, but obviously when it comes to new audiences, there is always a hill to climb. For a long time, this didn't worry me too much at all. I took an approach of, "Oh well, the people who are drawn to it will be drawn to it, and those who don't get it just won't get it, and I'm good with that." You can't be all things to all people.

There was a time, though, when I first moved to the US, where I started doubting myself and wondering whether I was being too dogmatic and stubborn. Everyone had an opinion. "Your name is the best! Keep it—it makes you stand out!" "It's terrible! So derogatory to women! You'll never make it here!"

I started seriously thinking that we should change the name for the American market, so we engaged a brand agency out of Los Angeles to begin the work. It was an arduous task that took months and months. Every two weeks, we'd jump on a call with the branding agency and hear their latest round of brand name suggestions. I had a minimum of three execs on every call. Calculate the cost of that, based on their hourly rate, plus my time, and it really adds up. Every two weeks, we'd be disappointed with what was coming back. It wasn't from a lack of trying on the agency's behalf. They had their top people on our account and were pulling out all the stops to come up with a name. They just weren't hitting the mark, and none of the names felt right.

My team and I agonized over this project and the outcomes we were trying to achieve. We were too far in over our heads, having spent a huge amount of money to get to this point. I was starting to sense a bit of an attitude of, "Let's just choose the closest one, even if we don't like it, because we've spent the money now and come too far." I had to stop them all thinking like this, do a sense check, and lead them to see that there was no way we were going to change the name just because we'd dropped a ton of cash and invested a heap of time. If it didn't feel right, we couldn't make it feel right.

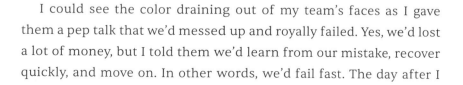

Failure is an event, not a person. Yesterday ended last night.
ZIG ZIGLAR

I could see the color draining out of my team's faces as I gave them a pep talk that we'd messed up and royally failed. Yes, we'd lost a lot of money, but I told them we'd learn from our mistake, recover quickly, and move on. In other words, we'd fail fast. The day after I made the decision not to change the name, I was over it. I'm not sure my CFO was, but I was!

JUST KEEP SWIMMING

Each year, I get the tough gig of heading to Necker Island with a bunch of our members for a leadership conference.

> ## When life gets you down, you know what you gotta do? Just keep swimming.
> ### DORY

Sir Richard Branson bought Necker Island to impress his girlfriend, now wife, Joan, many years ago. He transformed it into a luxury resort and playground, as well as a conservation haven for lemurs, flamingos, and dozens of other exotic creatures. A few years back, he also bought the island across from Necker (as you do), called Moskito.

Every now and then, Richard generously opens up Moskito for groups visiting Necker, as he kindly did for us. We were given the option to kayak, sail, stand-up paddleboard, motorboat, or swim across to Moskito. Being someone who never says no to a challenge, I chose the swim.

I'd swum from Necker to Moskito before, completely winging it as I'm not a swimmer. When I made it across back then, I made a vow to myself that I'd never do it again. Not that I didn't enjoy it, or feel a sense of accomplishment. I suppose I felt it was just one of those things in life that only needs to be done once. But here I was, attempting it again, and asking myself why.

This time, the swim was quite cathartic for me. As I set off from Necker Island and started on the two-and-a-half-mile journey, all I could think about was how similar it was to the journey of an entrepreneur.

First, you start out alone and ask yourself, "Why am I doing this again?" Then you find your rhythm, you gain momentum, and you think, "This is good. I'm heading in the right direction. I can do this." Really soon after, though, you start to get a bit tired and begin to doubt yourself. "I've got a long way to go. This is hard. Why am I doing this?" Then you start to feel very, very alone. You look behind you, and there's no one else there, and you look ahead, and there's no one there either. You realize that even though there are people who love and support you, the job of an entrepreneur is a lonely one.

The next part of the swim is the hardest. You wonder if you're getting anywhere, achieving anything. It's just stroke after stroke, hoping you're moving forward toward your goal. Just as you feel like you can't go any further, there's a glimmer of hope. A boat passes by, full of your people, and they yell out, "You can do it! You're doing so well! Woohoo!" and you feel buoyed by their encouragement. You swim faster and stronger, and you feel invincible. But soon that boat is out of sight and you're back being alone, and the water looks impossibly deep, and you start to think about sharks and stingrays and the unknown lurking beneath you.

If you're strong, you now dig deep, keep your head down, and keep going. You tell yourself you can do this. If you're not strong, you look for the support boat, wave to them, and they come and rescue you, which is what happened to one of my fellow swimmers. I felt bad for him and watched as he was pulled from the water, but it made me even more resolved to succeed.

Soon enough, the island you're heading toward comes into view. Suddenly, your goal seems possible. It's within reach. "You're almost there," you say to yourself. You lift your tired arms out of the water, one after the other, perhaps breaking for a second and looking for reassurance from the support boat. They nod in encouragement, and you start to feel like you just might have this.

And it turns out you do. The water becomes shallower and shallower, and the white sand starts to emerge. You think, "I can't believe I just did that." You stand up, a little shaky from the swim, and your people are there for the high fives and the celebration.

That swim was poignant for me, and the eternal question of how to succeed was answered (thanks, Dory): just keep swimming.

DON'T CALL ME SUPER-WOMAN

"Once on the trampoline, I wanted to do a flip
but I'd never done it before. I thought,
'Heck, I'll just give it a go.' And I did.
I was a bit scared at the start, but
then I did it, and it felt good."

MILLA ISAACS, AGE 10

IT'S REALLY, REALLY HARD

The most common question I get asked is how I do it all. There has never been an easier question to answer: I don't. I have six children, but I consider myself the most unprofessional mother you are ever likely to meet. While I researched birth, I barely researched parenting (thinking I'd figure it out somehow) and as a result, I'm winging it 95 percent of the time.

It took me three children to figure out that the markings on diapers changed from yellow to blue when they got wet. I've never been able to put up or collapse a stroller; I've always just made sure I had a car big enough to throw it in the trunk completely intact (hey, it saves time!). I go to IKEA with no real purpose just so I can get an hour's free babysitting at their play center, my kids have never had a Santa photo taken, and I call my friends every time those two lines appear on the pregnancy test: "But they're really, really faint, so I'm fine, right?"

Many a time, I have been late to the childcare pickup and copped a bunch of five-dollar fines for each minute I neglected them. I'm also partial to moving the kids' birthdays to when it's more convenient for me, and on a recent flight, traveling alone with my three-month-old baby girl, I managed to spray the businessman beside me with breast-milk as I was feeding her. Neither of us really knew what to do, but there was this sort of silent agreement not to make eye contact after that.

I'm guilty of all these parenting fails, and yet they don't matter at all. I've never been out to impress anyone other than my kids. I know I'm good at the stuff that matters—being there for endless cuddles, listening intently to their woes, gently encouraging and guiding, and trying to instill the values that I hope are going to best get them through life.

My grandmother raised six kids and worked full-time as a school principal. She was tough but fair, and we all adored her. Sadly, she passed away from ovarian cancer several years ago, which was even more devastating given she was still sharp as a tack and had so much to offer.

My sister and I visited her in the hospital, and at the time, we each had two children. A little exasperated from the task of modern-day parenting, we asked her, "Nanny, how did you ever do it with six?" She smiled and said, "I left them alone and told them to sort it out among themselves whenever there was a problem."

You could say she was the opposite of a helicopter parent, and I've taken a lot of my parenting cues from her. I don't over-parent my kids, just as I don't micromanage my team members. I don't wrap them in cotton wool or watch their every waking moment, just as I wouldn't stand over my team and watch as they execute a project. I believe we need to find more trust in ourselves and in others, and relax a whole heap more.

> ## Parenting is a lot like the bar scene: Everyone's yelling, everything's sticky, it's the same music over and over again, and occasionally someone pukes.
> ### UNKNOWN

In my experience, the most stressed parents are those who spend every moment hovering over their children and predicting their every move. It must be exhausting! It's also impossible to do when you have a bunch of kids. Of course, keeping our kids safe is paramount, but they need to find their independence too. They're going to fall, trip, and hurt themselves, and that's never fun, but it also teaches them that life is not all unicorns and rainbows.

I recently went to an event in Los Angeles with a panel of high-profile female entrepreneurs speaking. These women all happened to have children, so naturally the conversation turned to how they manage their families and business lives. On the question of juggling, none of them honestly acknowledged their own situations. On the question of balance, they made it appear effortless.

I left the event feeling deflated and not good enough, because none of these women really let us into their lives, including the type of help they get and the mistakes they've made as they navigate the parenting journey. The truth is, even though those women on the stage would have you think otherwise, it's really, really hard. You should never let anyone fool you into thinking they have it completely sorted.

No amount of Instagram filtering will mask the chaos

Now that I've got a few years of parenting under my belt, I feel it's my responsibility to tell the truth and paint an honest picture of what it's like to have a big family and take on what I do with my businesses.

If you're lucky enough to be a parent, you have these little people with their own sets of personalities and needs and wants, and what they need and want is most often in opposition to what *you* need and want. I mean, have you ever heard your kids ask for a bit of peace and quiet? A coffee? More sleep?

They want to go slow and sit and play with you when your caffeine has just kicked in and you're ready to smash your inbox. They want more food when you've just cleaned the kitchen and put everything away. And just as you've finally drifted off to sleep, a little hand will tap you on the shoulder wanting a glass of water, immediately stirring your mind into overdrive, taking you another full hour to get back to sleep. Every. Damn. Night.

No matter how much it might look like someone has it sorted, the truth is that no parent really does, even the so-called experts who always carry spare diapers and know how their stroller works. For every good Facebook picture, I can guarantee you there would have been thirty tantrums, bouts of sickness, and sleepless nights. I know you know this. I know it too. But every now and then, we can get sucked into believing that we're the only ones who don't know what we're doing.

I don't want to be seen as the person who has it all together. I live in a permanent state of roll call with my kids, checking their names off in my head to make sure I haven't lost one. My favorite game is hide-and-seek, because I can genuinely hide and have two minutes to myself. I'm often hatching plans of how I can get them all out of the house at once (it's been done!) so I can just sit on the end of the bed and observe the silence. I'm here to admit that I'm completely up and down with my parenting: I oscillate between never wanting to see them ever again and experiencing an intense craving to leave the office early and race home to hold them all.

All of this being said, I have to remember that I chose this, so it's impossible for me to play the victim about it. The children bring us joy and chaos in equal measure, and in a way, the kid thing has helped me lift my game and focus on what's most important, both at home and in my business.

The wasted emotion

I see a lot of parents struggling with guilt, and I've always believed it's a completely wasted emotion, where no one wins.

Over the past few years, living in Los Angeles and traveling back to Australia up to eight times a year, I've missed countless birthdays, school concerts, and field trips. While it's never easy, I refuse to let myself feel guilty for more than a few moments.

I've always been really clear in telling my kids why I work as much as I do. I always tell them that I'm not just working so we can take them on vacation to Hawaii or Mexico, or pay for the groceries each week. I tell them that I'm trying to create jobs, I'm trying to help and inspire women, and I'm trying to have an impact on the world.

I do feel guilt from time to time, but I don't suffer from it. Of course, it's hard to FaceTime with my four-year-old son when he starts to cry because he wants me but I'm still overseas, or when I have to shut my office door on one of the rare occasions I'm working at home, and my kids try to knock it down because they want to tell me something but I have to finish my conference call. A wave of guilt always comes over me, but then I let it go.

And that's because guilt is an emotion that keeps us stuck.

I snap myself out of guilt and feeling stuck as quickly as I can each time, and throw myself into another emotional state. I resolve to come up with a way to spend more time with the kids or move a meeting that's standing in the way of me getting to the next school concert.

I always try to replace my guilt with emotional honesty. I let the kids know that I'm doing my best, but that I also falter, and that I also find it hard to be away from them. I think what they want to know above all else is that they're heard and loved, and that I'm committed to learning and making it better for all of us.

It would be unnatural not to experience guilt on some level as a parent. It confirms to us that we care deeply about our children and we care deeply about our responsibilities as parents. I know I do. We all want the absolute best for our kids, but feeling guilty for leaving them at daycare, or for being on your phone while they're happily playing at the park, helps no one. If you're really unhappy about either of those things, then do something about it. Do anything. Don't just allow yourself to feel guilt and remain stuck there.

MY BRAND OF DOING IT ALL

There's an idea called the Four Burners Theory, where you imagine your life as a four-burner stove. Each burner represents friends, family, health, and work. It's been said that if you want to be successful, you have to turn off at least one of your burners. And if you want to be super-successful, you need to turn off at least two.

For the past few years, my work and family burners have been turned up to the point you'd experience third-degree burns if you got close. My friends and health burners are simmering, if not completely turned off.

My health burner used to run hot. I had a personal trainer five mornings a week, squeezed in a few yoga and aerobics classes, played on the work netball team, and consulted with a Reiki master and a kinesiologist.

These days, I'm lucky to make a quick green smoothie each morning. Occasionally I'll lift the odd kettlebell, usually when I trip over it in the closet and am reminded it's there. I turn down most social engagements, choosing instead a small handful of friends who understand I'm not a Saturday-morning-long-brunch-and-coffee friend anymore, but more a ten-minute-quality-conversation-on-the-fly-between-meetings-in-the-back-of-an-Uber kind of friend.

Because my work and family burners are turned up so high, I find that what works at the moment is to be gentle with myself. I focus on my mental health over my physical health. I prioritize how I'm feeling, how I manage stress, and my mindset. I also know that where I'm at right now is just a moment in time and I'll be able to turn those other burners back up soon enough.

And that's my brand of doing it all right there—I don't. I do work and family really well, have a bunch of forgiving friends, and take the stairs when I can.

My advice on doing work and family well

I feel lucky that I started my entrepreneurial journey very early on. Before I became a mom, I'd already collected a bunch of useful skills from business that became helpful in parenting.

When it comes to running my household and my business, the same rules apply. Get good people around you. Have fun. Watch your body language, and watch your mood too. Move fast when required, and slow when needed. Create a fun environment. Stay calm. Don't take yourself too seriously. And perhaps most important, get organized.

In a way, having six children was a game I challenged myself with. It costs a bucketload to provide for them, educate them, and travel with them (you can imagine when we fly anywhere how much the eight plane tickets cost, and we always need a minimum of two hotel rooms when we go on vacation). I knew that having a big family would be expensive so I'd either have to learn how to play big or simply not get ahead.

DO separate your two roles as much as possible, if you're serious about getting ahead in your career and being a great parent. When you're busy being a parent, do that well. When you're working, work. Working from home has never really worked for me, as I'd always find something that would take me away from focusing on what I need to get done, so it's something I've tried to avoid.

DON'T say you can't afford help. There are a ton of ways you can get a little or a lot of it. Consider family daycare or the number of coworking spaces that are popping up with daycare facilities, or an au pair program. Some of my friends even share an au pair and find that works for them. Could you even employ a babysitter for a few hours a week and discipline yourself to do the most pressing priority during that time? Childcare is an expensive, age-old challenge with no easy fix. It is important though to try and work out some solutions and not give up. I've seen people give up way too quickly, saying, "That didn't work for us." Try again! Try something new! Keep trying until you've found what works for you and your family.

DO work really hard on your relationships with the people who help care for your kids. Over the years, we've been so lucky to have people in our family who adore our kids as much as we do. These caregivers (whether they're at the local preschool or working as a nanny in our home) are family to us. We try to be as kind and generous as we can, always thanking them and looking for ways to show our appreciation. It may just be an unexpected gift voucher to a movie or spoiling them on their birthdays, but it's so important to acknowledge the work they do.

DON'T try to do it all at once. Having six kids has made Rowan and me experts in dividing and conquering. He'll take three and go do an activity, and I'll have the other three doing something else. We've always just found this easier. I'll never forget one time we were all catching a plane together. As we were clearing security, the kids collected their bags off the conveyer belt and pretty much went in five different directions while I was trying to manage the baby. I looked at Row and said, "See, I told you we'd have been better splitting up and taking a couple each!"

DO create opportunities for one-on-one time with your children. I do this all the time. Taking them out for lunch on the weekends or after school can go a long way toward filling up their emotional cup. Sometimes I grab one of them and take them to a hotel for the night, where we watch a movie that they choose, or read books, or just snuggle and talk a lot. It need not be a hotel, either—sometimes, if the hours in the day run out, I'll sneak one of them into our bed and they'll spend the night there with us.

DON'T apologize for your ultra-organization. Come to my place in the evenings, after the kids' bedtime, and you're going to find four lunch boxes lined up for the kids who go to daycare/school on the kitchen bench in age order. You're going to find a chopping board in the same place every night, ready for prep the next day, four cups on the breakfast table ready to be filled with water the next morning, half the lunch boxes already filled with nonperishables, water bottles ready to go, backpacks lined up on their hooks just outside the kitchen (again, in age order), and so it goes. The systems set you free. They give you time to manage the stuff you can't control or predict—hello, sibling arguments.

DO be present. A skill I've tried to master is really being present wherever I am and doing what matters. I don't have the hours available to me that I used to have, so when I'm in the office, I try to spend time in the "important and not urgent" quadrant. When I'm at home, I'm doing the stuff that matters too—being present with the kids, cuddling them, reading to them, and listening (really listening) to them. I try to let everything else fade into the background. I fail regularly, but the goal is to always be working when I'm working and parenting when I'm parenting.

DO always have something to look forward to as a family. The monotony and routine of day-to-day family life can feel like there's just no end in sight. You feel as though you're in an endless cycle of managing disagreements, missing out on sleep, making meals that only get half-eaten, tidying up, and getting zero time for yourself. We always try to have something on the calendar that we're looking forward to, usually a family vacation or another big event. We count down the days together, and it helps remind us that there's a light at the end of the tunnel.

DO understand how you get your energy. Energy is probably the most critical superpower to harness in parenting and business (and life, really!). When you have energy and you're in the right headspace, dealing with a toddler tantrum is bearable. When you're running on empty, it feels like an insurmountable mountain to climb. I know that I get my energy from being alone. Sometimes, all I need is half an hour to be away from every human in the world. I'll turn to Row and say, "Please just take them all in the car and drive around for a little while!" The minute they're piled into the car and the door closes, I'll make coffee (or a glass of wine, if it's late enough in the day), or get in the shower, or even just sit on the edge of my bed and stare out the window. By the time they come back, I love them all again. You may not be an introvert like me and recharge by being alone. Maybe you're one of those cool people who recharges their batteries by being around others. The point is: know how you get energy and make sure you allow time to get more of it.

DON'T ever begrudge your partner's time out. I love it when Row goes away, even for just a day or two, and he feels the same about me. While it can be tricky managing on your own, it allows your partner to do what they love and gives them the space to miss you all too. And having at least one reenergized parent in the house is always better than two exhausted ones!

DO find family rituals. We love taking our bikes down to the beach and riding along the boardwalk. And Friday night dinner is also a must.

DO buy in bulk, or at least buy two of everything. When I buy diapers, I buy stacks. There's no running out in my house, ever. Same goes for baby wipes and soap and toilet paper. And everything else, basically. All of this is not to say I'm flippant with waste, because I'm not. I recycle everything and work hard to keep packaging down and do my best to tread lightly, but if you want to make life easier, avoid at all cost having to go to the store because you've run out of something.

DO set up stations all over the place. When I buy a hairbrush for the kids, I buy two. Same goes for hair detangler spray and hair elastics. I buy three pairs of scissors at a time and have all these things stationed all over the house—in the bathroom, in our bedroom, in the kitchen. The name of the game is to be able to get your hands on things as quickly as possible and never waste a minute more on looking for stuff than you have to.

DO delegate decisions. This may boggle your mind, but humans make approximately 35,000 decisions a day. No wonder we're all so strung out and stressed! I'll never forget the day I decided to stop making as many decisions in my household. Our nanny said to me, "What should I make for dinner for the kids?" Of course, this was completely well meaning, but something just kind of snapped in me. I'd come off a particularly intense New York work trip, and I was tired. My husband was in the kitchen when the nanny asked this question. Very calmly I just said to them both, "You know what, guys? This is the last night I'm ever going to decide what to feed the kids for dinner unless it's my turn to cook. I make far too many decisions all day in my business to have any space left for more of them when I get home." Thankfully, my husband picked up what I was putting down, and he spent that night collating a book of recipes that we can all use to feed the kids.

DON'T be a hoarder. I try to live as simply and lightly as possible and make sure our home is not cluttered. I don't buy a lot of new stuff for the kids either. That's what grandparents are for. I'll regularly clean out the kids' clothes and toys and donate everything to charities. Also, make sure you have heaps of storage to hide the clutter.

DO buy everything online. It's safe to say I'm one of Amazon's best customers. There's not much I don't buy online. If a birthday invitation comes home in a school backpack one day, I'm online that night sorting the gift out.

I don't have all the answers, but I know life is easier because we don't sweat the small stuff. We're very chill with how things run in our house. We'll often dance on tables, have food fights, eat ice cream when we're not meant to, and just let our kids be kids. I'm strict on some stuff (no screens during the week, for example), but 95 percent of the time our kids are free-range, and life is as fun as we can make it.

"IT'S CANCER," THEY SAID

When my eldest child, Milla, was four, I noticed a small lump on her neck. At first, I thought nothing of it. Glands go up and down. Over the next few months, I kept checking the lump, and it kept growing. Worried, we took her to the doctor, who assured us there was nothing wrong and we should just continue to monitor it. Months passed and one day as I was giving her a hug, I could have sworn it had visibly grown. The next day, we took her back.

The doctor referred us to the children's hospital, where we underwent some tests. Milla had a biopsy and numerous scans done. The results came in, and our worst fears were confirmed: Milla had cancer.

There's no textbook to tell you how to react when you're told your baby has cancer. The one that I've written in my head for my life so far goes a little something like this: stay calm, stay grateful, and be generous. So we decided to do just that. But first, we'd have to get through everything that comes with a cancer diagnosis.

Those first few days and weeks after Milla's diagnosis are all a bit of a blur. Of course I was listening to what the doctors were saying, but I was having an out-of-body experience at the same time. There was so much information to take in, and I was trying to keep up with it all, as I knew our parents would have so many questions for us and I wanted to be able to answer them as best I could.

Our doctor explained that Milla had Hodgkin's lymphoma. Hodgkin's lymphoma can occur at any age, but it's most common in adolescents and young adults. It's a rare disease, accounting for half a percent of cancers, and there are only around thirty young people from birth to age fourteen who are diagnosed with it each year in Australia.

On the day we found out, I remember picking Milla up from daycare early. I'm not even sure if I told the staff why. I was generally one of the last parents to pick up their kid each day, trying to squeeze every minute possible out of my available working hours.

> **When something bad happens, you have three choices. You can either let it define you, let it destroy you, or you can let it strengthen you.**
> **UNKNOWN**

We went down to the beach so Milla and Honey (her sister, who was two at the time) could run around, and Row and I could have some space away from them to talk. I will never forget that afternoon. It was a hot, sunny day, and Milla ran ahead. Her long golden hair shone so brightly in the sunlight. It was only natural to project into the future and imagine what it would be like if all that beautiful hair was gone.

The oncologist wasted no time. She asked to see us the very next day, so in we went. It was our first time in the children's cancer ward and it was a sobering sight. The kids were in varying stages of treatment, most of them with no hair and all with sunken eyes and puffy faces. The parents all had the same worn looks on their faces. We must have looked all bright-eyed and bushy-tailed that first day. We had woken up with resolve and were ready to face whatever lay ahead with our usual determination.

We presented ourselves at the desk and told the clerk that we were there for our consultation with the oncologist. After some minutes of searching, he was adamant that he couldn't find our appointment. We were perplexed, and what he said next completely floored us. "No, I don't have you for an appointment today. All I have here is your surgery that's been booked for tomorrow, and the chemotherapy, which will start straight after that." Rowan and I looked at each other, and the tears welled up. Up until then, we had had no idea what Milla's treatment would be. I suppose we were hoping that she would have an operation to remove the lump in her neck where the cancer was found and that might just be it. Hearing that she was up for chemo was a whole different ball game.

Treatment was confronting and overwhelming. Milla went through two rounds of chemotherapy. Navigating all of that left our family paralyzed at times. I can't tell you how many times I lay in the bed next to Milla with tears streaming down my face. I wasn't sobbing or making a sound, but the tears just would not stop. I was wishing with all of my heart that it was me going through it and not her.

The first time that Row and I had to administer the oral chemo drugs was horrific. To start with, there were numerous medications, and we needed to concentrate hard and consult with each other over dosages and timings. It felt like another business to run. Here was this activity that had taken over our lives and forced us into competency really quickly. Unlike business, though, Milla's life depended on this, so there wasn't room for error or sloppiness. We soon settled into a routine that involved drugs, tests, consultations, appointments, and more drugs. I would marvel at (and lose sleep over) how toxic Milla's body had become.

Looking back on all this, I realize now that I was numb for most of it, just doing whatever we needed to survive. Now, though, whenever I think about what she went through, I feel a pang of sadness. Milla, being the eldest, and having inherited far too much of my independence and resilience, coped like a trouper, but she was also forced to grow up way too fast. When I think about that time, I can't help but resent that a little piece of her childhood and innocence was snatched away from her.

Amid the awfulness, however, we found so much to be thankful for. We met some beautiful souls during those days—social workers, psychiatrists, nurses, and doctors—all of whom were world-class and took a huge amount of care and interest in Milla. There was one young woman, Amy, who saved the day many a time. Amy always seemed to pop up at the right time with a bunch of stickers for Milla, or a picture and some pencils. Whenever a cannula needed to be put in, or when Milla wanted to eat something after twelve hours of fasting but couldn't ("But I'm starving, Mommy, please!"), I'd ask the nurses to track down Amy, and she'd always appear. Her calm, patient, understanding way was a constant source of comfort to us.

On the day of Milla's final chemotherapy treatment, Row and I sat on either side of her, holding her hands, and wiping away her tears, all of which seemed a little more bearable on this day, knowing that we were almost there. While the chemo was being administered, we looked up to find every nurse and doctor on the ward converging into the tiny room and huddling around Milla's bed. They were all wearing party hats and had musical instruments and they sang a "Happy End of Treatment" song and gave Milla gifts. While Milla beamed at the attention, the same tears flowed from me as they had on that day of Milla's very first treatment—silent tears that I couldn't control. I was so grateful for these wonderful people who had served us with so much skill and compassion. It was a strange feeling to think that I would miss seeing them, but nothing could replace the elation I was feeling that this nightmare would be over soon.

While I would not for a second wish a cancer diagnosis upon any child and their family, Milla's ordeal was the greatest gift our family has ever received. For me, it recalibrated everything we had to be grateful for. Row and I had the independence and ability to take as much time as we needed off work, and we had the financial means to have our two other children looked after (by the end of the treatment, I'd had our third baby, Indie) while we spent the time with Milla.

During treatment, Milla's focus was often on others rather than herself. I would see her climb down gingerly from her hospital bed, wearing only a pair of underpants, with tubes connected into her little chest pumping chemicals into her tiny body, and wheel the attached IV drip over to a kid who was having a hard time across from her. She'd stand there and comfort them. One time, I overheard her saying, "You want to escape with me? Why don't we just fly on out of here together?" She was so tender and thoughtful, just trying to lighten the load for the other kids, even though she was going through her own pain.

During this time, I learned that kids have a tremendous capacity for resilience. They can deal with what's in front of them at the time, and they're not wondering what happens in the future. They're very much in the here and now.

Any time life or business gets challenging, I have this experience to draw from. Milla taught us that if you can get through what she did, you can pretty much get through anything. And when you've been through something like we did with Milla, you very quickly lighten up about piles of laundry, messy bedrooms, and everything else that comes with everyday parenting.

MONEY IS NOT A DIRTY WORD

"It was the winter of 1977, I was nineteen and living in the UK, and it was freezing cold. I was reading the Sunday paper looking for the hottest place on earth and saw that it was 107 degrees in Johannesburg, South Africa. As I turned the page, there was an advertisement from the South African government looking for beauty therapists, and six weeks later I was on a flight to Johannesburg. If I hadn't taken that flight, I wouldn't have met my husband and moved to Los Angeles four years later to start our own business."

JANE WURWAND
founder, Dermalogica

IT'S NOT WHAT YOU EARN, IT'S WHAT YOU DO WITH IT

Over the years, I've become very clear on why money matters to me. I have no interest in accumulating more stuff or being showy about what I've created. I'm interested in how I can reduce stress and also create a great life for my family, but more important, I'm interested in how I can be generous and what I can do to make an impact somehow in the world.

A few years ago, I surprised my mom with a new car for her birthday. It had been a dream of mine to buy her one for many years; Mom is so selfless that she'd never buy one for herself. I had the salesperson wrap it in a huge red bow and deliver it to my house, where my mom was staying for the weekend, wrangling kids and laundry. I asked her to come down the driveway, where we had it waiting for her, and I'll never forget how surprised she was when she worked out what was going on. It gave me such joy to see the happy tears rolling down her face.

Getting your relationship with money right is crucial. We're often taught through the messages we receive that having money is a bad thing and that only greedy people care about money. This couldn't be further from the truth. The moment I got clear on what money could do for my life and, more important, what it could do for others, was the moment the abundance started flowing.

It's all about mindset

When it comes to money and personal finance lessons, there are two rules I live by. The first is that it's all about mindset: you have to believe you're worthy enough to be financially independent, or wealthy, if that's your goal.

My grandfather, who we call Poppy, is eighty-seven and is my biggest role model when it comes to building wealth. A boat builder by trade, who never earned more than a very modest wage, he was defiant in his approach to wealth creation. His motto was "Small actions over a long

"Money is fun to make, fun to spend,
and fun to give away."

SARA BLAKELY

period of time add up." Every month, he'd walk into the city branch of his bank and hand over his mortgage payment in cash. Through this monthly ritual he got to know all of the tellers on a first-name basis. He tells me how he'll never forget the very last mortgage payment he made, striding proudly into the branch with a big smile on his face and letting everyone know that he'd never see them again.

Poppy, while paying off his mortgage, also took an interest in the stock market. He would only buy blue-chip stocks and he'd never be tempted to sell them off. He'd also reinvest the dividends instead of taking out the profits, and it's fair to say that Poppy has done really well over the years.

Still, you buy Poppy undies for Christmas and ten years later they'll be sitting in his drawer, unopened in the original packet.

Start early

The second rule is that the earlier you start, the better off you'll be. During my teenage years, my dad got interested in one of those multilevel marketing schemes. As a result, our home was suddenly filled with personal development books, videos, and cassettes. If my dad was dropping me off at a sports game, we'd listen to Tony Robbins or Zig Ziglar, and on the way to school it might have been Robert Kiyosaki. I caught religion right then and there. These teachers appealed to me. They were real-life examples of what hard work could get you. They taught me that you didn't need to be born into huge wealth or have a formal education to get ahead. If it was possible for them, I was going to make it possible for me.

I couldn't learn enough. I was so hungry for knowledge. And even though there were hardly any women teaching these courses or being featured in these magazines, I knew I could do it.

Napoleon Hill's *Think and Grow Rich* was my favorite book. I remember one part where Hill writes, "The poor man looks at the big house on the hill and says, 'I can't afford that' and the rich man looks at the big house on the hill and says, 'How can I afford that?'" I remember reading that line over and over and really letting it sink in.

I had lots of problems initially getting a mortgage. I'm sure my age deterred most lenders, as did my measly wage, and I only had a 10 percent deposit so I had to pay mortgage insurance. I got turned down by eight different mortgage brokers before the ninth one said yes. The rejection hurt, but I wouldn't let it get to me. I just kept going until eventually one agreed to give me a loan (and I kept all the rejection letters as a reminder to never take no for an answer).

I was nineteen when I bought my first property. It was a two-bedroom, off-the-plan apartment in a small development of only twelve condos. For me, it ticked all the boxes. It was close to public transport, shops, and schools, and although it was in a relatively dodgy area, I knew that the suburb and the value of my apartment would have to improve over time.

When I finally got that mortgage, I was like a bull terrier. I got obsessed. I lived to pay it down. I took out one of the rejection letters, and I drew up a makeshift spreadsheet on the back. It was a very simple chart, with only three columns. Across the top I wrote "Date," "Amount Paid Off," and "New Mortgage Amount."

If my grandfather gave me fifty dollars for my birthday, I'd go straight to the bank and put that fifty dollars toward the mortgage. If I got a surprise tax return, I wouldn't go shopping with it—I'd put it toward the mortgage. If Uber had been around back then, I would have switched on the app and become a driver at every available moment. Whatever it took. Before I knew it, I was making headway. The year after, I was able to buy my second investment property, a tiny little studio apartment in inner Sydney. I still own both of those properties, twenty years after I bought them.

Years after I started my property investment journey, Mark Bouris, founder of Wizard Home Loans, spoke for Business Chicks. After his speech, as we were standing in front of the media wall posing for a picture, I shook his hand and told him that he'd missed out on a great customer in me. He asked what I meant, and I told him that his business had rejected me for a mortgage when I was a very keen nineteen-year-old and that I had gone on to amass a decent-sized property portfolio since. He chuckled and apologized that his company hadn't backed me. I told him there was no need to say sorry, as it was his loss, and we had a good laugh together.

The misconception about wealth creation

People think you have to earn a lot of money to start investing, but it's not true. If you're consistent with your savings and investing, and start as soon as possible, you can really create some magic. There are countless stories of people who earn huge salaries but also live beyond their means and have nothing left over to show for it. Compare that to my grandfather, who earned a mediocre wage but was thrifty and astute, and I know which story I'd choose for myself.

I know how intimidating it can be to get your financial house in order, so here are some tips and tricks to help you along the way.

START YOUNG, BUT MORE IMPORTANT, JUST START. Choosing to start investing so young was a real gift for my future business life. Banks love collateral, as it means that if you need a commercial loan or line of credit, you're going to be far more attractive to a lender than if you have no assets. If you're no spring chicken, then that's fine too; just start small and start wherever you are!

LIVE WITHIN YOUR MEANS. I try to spend money on things that are important to me, and I'm conscious about what I spend, always asking whether I really need the item or not. My kids talk in the "Do we really need this, or do we just want it?" language now too.

THE WORST THING YOU CAN DO IS NOTHING. Don't suffer from fear or inertia, hoping that any financial problems will just go away, because they won't. Take baby steps toward making it different today. My husband and I sit down regularly to talk about our finances. It's not always a comfortable chat, but we do it anyway. We talk about what's coming up, what we're investing in, where the potential roadblocks might be, and how we can better our situation.

GET A WEALTH MENTOR TO GUIDE YOU. I've mentioned my wonderful assistant, Britt, who helped me to manage my investment properties a few years back, among a million other tasks. When it came to property, she asked me lots of questions about how I got started and what she'd need to do to get the same results. I was so happy when she called me a year after we'd stopped working together to tell me that she'd done it—she'd bought her first property! She said she would never have been able to do it if she hadn't been exposed to my experiences. Can you think of someone who could mentor you in the same way?

CHOOSE A MONEY BUDDY. If you can't access an experienced wealth mentor, at least find a friend who you can meet up with every now and then to share their money goals and keep you accountable for yours. I've found that most people don't like discussing money, but I also know that what gets focused on gets results.

USE YOUR CASH WISELY. If you're lucky enough to have a surplus of cash, then use those funds strategically. It's one thing to have a safety stash saved up for a rainy day, but there's also no point in having a ton of money sitting in the bank and not working hard for you. A few years back, we had a killer year. We'd managed costs really well, focusing on strong, profitable activities, and it paid off. I could have easily bought myself something flashy, but instead I chose to invest in the business and purchase an office, where our company is now based.

DON'T RELY ON ONE INCOME STREAM. It's said that a typical millionaire has, on average, seven income streams. You may not need seven, but thinking about how you can create multiple income streams could be a game changer.

DON'T GET ATTACHED. Investment needs to be unemotional. With my investment properties, I don't care if I like them or not; I care what the numbers tell me. What matters is if they're attractive to tenants, offer strong rental returns, and achieve capital growth.

"A GOOD PLAN VIOLENTLY EXECUTED NOW IS BETTER THAN A PERFECT PLAN EXECUTED NEXT WEEK." I love this quote by George S. Patton, and it applies to most aspects of life, especially your finances. Sometimes making fast decisions with investing is the way to go, rather than trying to predict the market and time it perfectly. I have a friend who's been telling me for over twenty years now that it's not the right time to buy property. In those twenty years, I've been busy investing, and meanwhile he's stuck just owning one property (his home) and continues to wait for the "right time" to come along.

HAVE A SPEND-FREE DAY ONCE A WEEK. I once set myself the challenge of having at least one day each week where I didn't spend a cent. It was tough at first, but then it became clear how much incidental and mindless spending we do. When you have a spend-free day, you have to get creative about a few things: how you will get to the office and what you will take in for lunch, for example. It just makes you that little bit more organized and brings a consciousness to your spending.

THE ONE THING YOU NEED TO TAKE VERY SERIOUSLY

When it comes to business finances, this is the one area of my life where I definitely don't "wing it" in the truest sense of the phrase.

Growing a financially healthy business requires you to continually work on your mindset and have a lot of courage. There have definitely been times when I've just had to say, "Screw it, it will be okay," and take a leap of faith. But, generally speaking, I am incredibly astute and careful when it comes to how quickly I grow my company and manage our funds.

We've been in challenging cash flow situations many, many times and it's always difficult to manage through those times. The one thing I've learned is to not stick my head in the sand, and to work out a plan the second I learn that we're moving into dangerous territory. If money is going to run out in two months, money is going to run out in two months. Every day spent ignoring the problem creates more angst and pressure.

A few years back, things got fairly close to the wire and I had to sell two investment properties. It wasn't fun, but it was necessary. I gritted my teeth, made a strong decision, and moved us forward. That process took a couple of months in itself. Had I hesitated when I discovered the cash flow problem, it would have been too late. That was the first time I had ever sold a property, so I felt a sense of failure that it had come to that. But I knew it was the right decision. It got us out of a tight spot and also allowed us to leapfrog into the next stage of growth.

It goes without saying that financial acumen is so important in business. It's one of the traits that can make or break you and, thankfully, it's a skill that you can learn (and hallelujah for that, because I well and truly sucked at math in school).

Knowing your financial position, getting clear on your financial philosophy, and understanding your risk appetite are paramount. That might sound like a really simple statement, but a lot of people still don't know how to pull the levers to make more money when it's required.

In the early days, it was up to me to watch the cash like a hawk and work out how we were doing. These days, I invest heavily in having the right people (inside and outside of my business) who can spend time with the numbers and report back on our results, but I still always know how we're placed.

When it comes to business finances, these are the rules I live by.

START WITH THE END IN MIND. I'll never start a business without having at least an inkling of how I might eventually sell it.

CHECK YOUR CASH POSITION EVERY SINGLE DAY. Not a day goes by when I don't check my bank balances and understand exactly where we are, cash-wise.

GET INTO A FINANCIAL RHYTHM. Meet regularly with the people in your business and those helping manage it externally (advisors, planners, accountants, etc.) to discuss your financial position.

LEARN TO SAY NO. We can all work ourselves into a position where we're really busy, but the wheels are just spinning. Focus on the activity that makes you money, and say no to the activities that don't.

DON'T STOP UNTIL YOU GET A YES. If a bank says no to credit or a loan, ask them why. Ask what it would take for them to back you. Understand where they're coming from and what they need for their credit department to be able to say yes.

BE FIRM WITH YOUR PAYMENT TERMS. It surprises me how many businesses are lax when it comes to their payment terms. Control your debtors closely, because it's better that the money be sitting in your account earning interest than in theirs. Besides, you did the work or sold the product, so you've earned it! Check when payments are due, and don't ever be shy about chasing overdue payments. I've been known to follow up with debtors when my team hasn't had any luck, and I'm not embarrassed about that. Your business relies on the strength of your cash flow, and carrying debtors for months can unravel a company very quickly.

MASTER THE BASICS. You don't have to become a CPA to be able to read your financial statements. If you're starting out, ask your bookkeeper or accountant for some help, and don't be scared to admit that this is new territory for you.

LEARN TO FALL IN LOVE WITH YOUR BUSINESS FINANCES. Good energy attracts good energy! Just like with your personal finances, don't stick your head in the sand when it comes to your company's financial situation.

IF YOU HAVE EXCESS CASH, PUT IT SOMEWHERE ELSE. We have high-interest-bearing accounts where we park money when we're not using it. Every little bit counts!

REVENUE IS FOR VANITY; PROFIT IS FOR SANITY. It can be exciting to watch your business grow, and your annual revenues are a great barometer for success. However, a lot of people are fixated on their gross sales and don't focus on net profit results. Posting huge revenues is not the goal; having a strong bottom line is.

PAY YOURSELF. For those of you already in established businesses, let's talk for a minute about what you're taking home. If you're paying yourself somewhere on par with what you could get at a similar job outside your company, then you don't have a business. You have a job. And I can't think of anything worse than having a job in my own business. All that stress and heartache and the sleepless nights, all to receive what you could receive elsewhere without the stress? No thanks. Pay yourself generously first, and if you can't do that, then consider if you really have a viable business.

NEVER PAY INTEREST ON YOUR CREDIT CARDS. That's just wasted money. Be sure to create systems so you're reminded when payments are due.

WORK YOUR CREDIT CARDS TO YOUR ADVANTAGE. In our business, we travel a lot. It makes sense to have credit cards that earn frequent-flyer miles. If you're nifty with admin, apply for a couple and keep them around for the minimum term, then close them. This will help you really build up the points. Just be aware that this will affect your credit rating, and there'll be a bunch of other terms, such as a minimum spend amount, but if you're savvy, you can easily work the system to your advantage.

FIND FREE MONEY. Take the time to research and apply for government grants where you can. A quick Google search will help you find the ones that might apply to your business, or there are plenty of consultants whose job it is to help you find grants and manage you through the application process.

Two is better than one

I've always favored businesses that have at least two types of income streams: annuity and project income. Having annuity income means that you've worked out a way to make money while you sleep—the type of money that trickles in whether you work for it or not. Music artists are a good example of this: they receive royalties from their past work, so each time their song is played, they inch a tiny bit closer to financial freedom.

Project income is completely controlled by you: you can choose to turn the tap on by working harder, or turn it off when you can't manage it. Real estate companies are a classic example of the annuity and project income model. Most have a rental roll, so they collect the rents for their landlord clients and get paid a commission on this. Their project income is earned when they sell a property. Music artists may choose to tour or release a new album, which is their way of earning project income.

I had the annuity and project income model working beautifully with my recruitment company. Every week, we'd have temps out working for us, and our clients would pay their wages plus the statutory costs, including a commission for our agency. That revenue trickled in each week, whether we really worked for it or not. Our project income came from the permanent placements we made.

When I bought Business Chicks, the business model was shot. Actually, to be frank, there was no business model. What existed was a small brand and a template for running events that ostensibly made no money. They'd have an event, make some ticket sales, and then do it again a few months later. There were a few sponsors in the mix, but they were largely contra arrangements so although they were valuable, they were not going to pay wages. I knew this model wasn't sustainable and that we'd be in a constant state of feast or fast if I didn't change it. I agonized over the business model for months, working out ways we could achieve other revenue streams and really try to monetize the offering.

These days, our revenues come from annuity income (in the form of memberships and rolling sponsorships) and also project income (sponsor/brand campaigns, events, digital advertising, etc.). Forecasting is a lot easier, and cash flow is a whole heap less bumpy too.

THE
PEOPLE
EQUATION

"Once upon a time I was a children's party host, dressing up as a fairy or cheerleader and hosting disco parties. One day the guy who hosted all the boys' parties didn't show up for work. We had a party starting in five minutes, and the little boy whose birthday it was desperately wanted Batman to host the party.

Without thinking, I said I'd do it! And the next thing I knew, I was in a Batman suit, speaking in a Batman voice to thirty kids. It was a long three hours, but who knew I'd be such a great Batman?! I wouldn't have if I'd just sat in my little fairy/cheerleader bubble."

BREAHNA BETLEM
Events Executive, Business Chicks,
former fairy/cheerleader/Batman

THE KEY TO HIRING WELL

If you run a business, or work in a business with an entrepreneurial culture, you'll likely attract people who aren't interested in rules, who want to create something worth talking about, who don't have time to lose, and who think creatively. I don't know about you, but these are the sorts of people I want to hang out with!

I need people on my team who are going to wing it with me. These are the people constantly questioning the way things are done and trying to find ways to make life better. They don't just sit back and join the masses or happily wait in line. They're forever contemplating how to make life make more sense, and they aren't scared to start a conversation about what they'd do differently if they were in charge. It won't surprise you that these people also don't clock on and clock off on the dot of your office hours either.

We've hired people in our business before who absolutely hate uncertainty. They crave policy, procedure, rules, guidelines, and structure. They've called us disorganized, all over the shop, and other names that hurt at the time. We've tried to bend our shape and make them fit because these people are smart, talented, and have a lot to offer. It never works, though, because ultimately the business we run is a business that values creativity and ideas and innovation and challenging the status quo more than it values a color-coded calendar and six set meetings a day.

The people I try to hire are the ones who don't need to know how their day is going to go and have it mapped out to the minute. They're not going to break out in hives when you throw them a curveball and say, "I know you were focusing on x, but y has come along and now it needs our attention." They're the say-yes-figure-it-out-later types, and they see opportunities rather than problems in every situation. They're okay in an environment of uncertainty and, above all, they believe that optimism always finds a way.

People with true entrepreneurial spirit will also be able to show you that they've taken calculated risks in their lives and prove that they can execute, which is the most important skill an entrepreneur can have. No point having all the ideas in the world if you're not willing and ready to jump in and get it done.

When it comes to people, I believe there's no quality more valuable than enthusiasm. I've found it to be the best tool in almost every situation, and there's no place where it won't be appreciated, whether you're greeting a salesperson in a store, applying for a job, or picking up a baby from their crib after a nap. Having a big smile, a spring in your step, and the right attitude is a winning combination, and will always be more important to me than where you've worked in the past or the experience you've collected along the way.

Being the competent people they are, the managers on my team are always conscientious about ticking the right boxes when hiring: Do they have valid experience? Do they know the software we use? Very little of this matters to me, though (except for the technical roles, where some of this questioning is necessary), and I'm always encouraging these leaders to look for something different. What matters to me is how much a person will add to the culture of the business and how much value they'll bring to the people already working in it.

I'll say to the hiring manager after the interview, "Were they sunshiney?" "Were they likeable?" "Did they appear kind?" "Did you want to spend more time with them?" I want to know that the person we're considering bringing onto the team is going to be a pleasure to be around, and that they'll add to the enjoyment of our existing team. Given that we're in the business of building community and making life better for our members, these things matter.

When someone interviews for a role on my team, I'm looking first for a few key things.

HOW THEY TREATED THE FIRST PERSON THEY CAME IN CONTACT WITH. After each interview, I'll always ask our receptionist how the candidate treated them. Were they polite? Did they seem calm or flustered? Did they immediately give off a good vibe, or did they project something else? These questions tell me how personable the candidate is and if they're going to treat everyone equally.

HOW THEY ENTERED THE ROOM. I'd never hire someone who walks in slowly, dragging their feet, with their shoulders hunched over. I'm not looking for the next Olympic sprinting champion, but I always want people who are eager and keen and who look like they're up for their next adventure.

HOW MUCH EFFORT THEY'VE PUT IN. You can tell the candidates who've done their homework and taken the time to understand how the business works. This doesn't matter because it makes my ego feel good; it matters because I want people on my team who care enough to do this.

HOW THEY FOLLOW UP. Most candidates won't follow up after their interview, but it makes a great impression when they do. It doesn't need to be long or elaborate—just an acknowledgment of our time and the opportunity to have interviewed with the company.

> ## I hire people who are brighter than me and then I get out of their way.
> ### LEE IACOCCA

I love hiring new people. It's a joy to be able to give someone a great opportunity that they'll love, and it's exciting to think of the value they'll bring to the business.

When I start a company, the first thing I do is build a team around me that doesn't rely on me. It takes some time, for sure, but I always start with the end goal in mind, and this is to build a strong asset who isn't dependent on me. The same goes if you're running a team in someone else's business.

The way I do this is by hiring people to do the jobs I'm not good at and the jobs that can be reasonably outsourced to someone else. I also look to hire people who are brighter, more organized, more astute, lovelier, or more capable than me and the rest of the business. I'm never intimidated by someone who has more experience or more knowledge than I do. It really drives me to learn from others and admit that I don't have all the answers! It's liberating and empowering all at once to have people around with deeper skills and knowledge.

Getting the right people has always been one of my top priorities. I get it wrong from time to time, but having come from a background of reading hundreds of résumés a day and conducting countless interviews, I've come to learn a trick or two about engaging brilliant people.

WHEN HIRING, CONSIDER YOUR TEAM AVERAGE. There are two questions I always ask myself when considering someone for a role on my team. The first is, "Will this person lift the average of the team, or will they bring it down?" My goal is to consistently send the average upward. The other question is, "Is this person an A-grade team player, or am I settling for second best?" My experience is that your gut never fails on this one. You know when you're trying to convince yourself that they tick all the caliber and suitability boxes but, really, you're cutting corners to just get someone into the role. Yes, it can be painful trying to fill a vacant position, but it hurts more when you make a wrong hire.

LOOK OUTSIDE OF JOB ADS. Good people hang out with good people. Years ago, I was looking for a new assistant. I approached one of the girls on my team, asking if she knew anyone, and her best friend ended up joining us, working alongside me for five years. I always try to exhaust my personal network first, and then look externally for great people.

HIRE SLOW. In the race to fill a position as quickly as possible and get a person on board, we can often choose speed over suitability. It's important to take time when hiring, ensuring you get to know the person as best you can, and making sure they're a fit for you. The best career advice that I've been given is to work with people you love. Life is too short to surround yourself with people who don't lift you (and your business) up.

FIRE FAST. We all know this, but it's something that so many of us struggle with. I know I do. And I know my leaders do too. The reality is that business is business, and if there's someone who's creating tension in your team and causing big distractions, or not doing their job, the impact is immeasurable. They have to go. As much as we all want to be liked, making these strong decisions is all part of being a leader.

Netflix has an interesting take on their firing policy. They only keep their highly effective people. The company's culture statement, which has been viewed more than 16 million times and was once described by Sheryl Sandberg as the most important document to come out of Silicon Valley, reads: "We model ourselves on being a team, not a family. A family is about unconditional love, despite your siblings' unusual behavior. A dream team is about pushing yourself to be the best teammate you can be, caring intensely about your teammates, and knowing that you may not be on the team forever."

BUILD A TALENT PIPELINE. In the same way all businesses need to be working to a sales pipeline, it's a great idea to think about building a pipeline for talent too. I have a lot of people in my world that I know will eventually work with us. We haven't found the right spot for them yet, but I keep in touch with these people in the hopes of offering them a place on the team in the future.

REWARD YOUR PEOPLE FOR BEING TALENT SCOUTS. Start a policy of rewarding your people if they bring someone onto the team. Even $500 can be a great incentive. It's a little bit like dating apps—the good prospects usually aren't there. You want to attract the people who aren't actively looking for work.

HIRE ROLE MODELS. I'm always looking for people who can be role models for others. I want inspiring people around us so that we can all learn in some way. Role models need not be the most senior or oldest people in your organization. Some of the best role models I've had have been younger people. They're getting up to interesting stuff and showing maturity beyond their years, and it's inspiring to watch how they handle themselves, tackle problems, and show up in the world.

MAKE THE FIRST DAY COUNT. Back when I owned the recruitment company and a new person would start with the business, I'd stay up the night before their first day and bake a cake. I'd decorate it in the same colors as our logo, and I'd write their name and a welcome message. On their first day, at afternoon tea time, I'd bring out the cake and gather the whole team together to welcome them.

I don't have the time to make cakes for everyone these days, but a new team member's first day in the office is still as important as ever. No matter what we do, we're trying to send the same message: our people matter, and we care deeply about them.

Over the years, I reckon we've mastered the art of making people feel like part of the team from the minute they walk in on the first day, and if there's one thing I definitely don't wing, it's the way we induct new staff members.

GET THE TEAM INVOLVED BEFORE THEY START. We always share the new employee's email address prior to their starting with us so our team can send them a note congratulating and welcoming them. That way, there's already a level of rapport there, and it's easier for them to put all those new faces to names on day one.

BE ORGANIZED. We always have the new person's business cards ready for them when they arrive. Not only does it send a message that we're professional, but it says, "We value you, and by the way, our standards are high, and we expect you to hit the ground running." No one's complained yet.

LET THEM BE LATE. We always ask our new peeps to start a little later on their first day (say, 9:30 a.m.), so we can make sure their department is ready and we can put any finishing touches on their welcome if needed. First days are information overload, and it's great if you can reduce this time down a bit for them.

LEAD FROM THE TOP. I always make sure a senior leader in the business writes a card to every new employee who starts in our company. This is always waiting on the newbie's desk when they arrive.

STAGE THE FUN. We don't just welcome them once in the morning. We'll always have gifts waiting for the new person, maybe a bunch of balloons and a bottle of champagne along with a card. From there, we might have flowers delivered throughout the day or afternoon tea to celebrate the new arrival.

PLAN OUT THE FIRST FEW DAYS. We have a structured induction program mapped out, so the new team member receives a thorough introduction to the business and gets to spend time with the department heads or anyone else they'll work closely with.

MAKE A GOOD FIRST IMPRESSION. Compare the above experience to a friend of mine who recently started a new role and hardly one person on the floor introduced themselves. You've got two very different experiences right there, and if given the opportunity, I know which workplace I'd choose.

MANAGING PEOPLE

The one thing that underpins culture is leadership. You can't have a good culture if you don't have good leadership. In fact, it's the thing that brings it undone the fastest.

Over the years, I've experimented with a ton of different work perks. You name it, I've tried it. It's been exciting to watch new workplace trends, and I've done my best to keep up with most of them. I had a nap room installed in the office and, for many years, we had a private chef come in and cook lunch for the team. We've also hired a masseuse to treat the team to weekly massages, and brought in yoga instructors and meditation experts to run classes. I've had stylists come in and talk about personal presentation. Each week, we stock the kitchen with all the essentials, from fresh fruit to herbal teas.

What I've learned, though, is that no amount of free fruit can build you a strong culture. These perks will help make your people feel appreciated for a moment, but they're not the reason people stay with your business and rave about it to their friends. Nothing can replace strong leadership. Nothing can replace a leader who demonstrates that they care and keeps showing up time and time again, leading by example and being grateful for the efforts of their people.

> When I talk to managers I get the feeling they're important. When I talk to leaders I get the feeling that I'm important.
> **ALEXANDER DEN HEIJER**

The best book I've ever read on people is *First Break All the Rules: What the World's Greatest Managers Do Differently* by Marcus Buckingham and Curt Coffman. It was written back in 1999, but it's still as relevant today as it was back then.

The authors studied over twenty-five years of research from within the Gallup organization, which included reviewing interviews with more than 80,000 employees. What they discovered were twelve key questions that measured the strength of an organization's people and took the pulse of employee engagement.

Those questions were:

- Do I know what is expected of me at work?
- Do I have the materials and equipment I need to do my work right?
- At work, do I have the opportunity to do what I do best every day?
- In the last seven days, have I received recognition or praise for doing good work?
- Does my supervisor, or someone at work, seem to care about me as a person?
- Is there someone at work who encourages my development?
- At work, do my opinions seem to count?
- Does the mission/purpose of my company make me feel my job is important?
- Are my coworkers committed to doing quality work?
- Do I have a best friend at work?
- In the last six months, has someone at work talked to me about my progress?
- This last year, have I had opportunities at work to learn and grow?

I can't tell you the number of times I've used these questions to help me figure out a people problem over the years, and when I do, the answers are usually clear as day. If someone is going off the rails a little bit, I refer back to these questions to see if they might give me clues about what's happening for them, and the questions never let me down.

Building an amazing culture

Your company culture is the set of values and beliefs that show the world, "This is how we do things around here." Creating an uplifting and performance-driven culture isn't an exact science, but when you get it right, everyone feels it.

In my first business, I wrote something I called a Culture Statement. It was a two-pager that we shared with newbies coming into the business, and it went a long way in articulating the culture we'd created and were striving to maintain. On one side, I wrote at the top, "What we expect from you," and on the other side I wrote, "What you can expect from us."

Some of the things we expected of our team were, "Admit when you've done something wrong," "Go above and beyond for your customers," and, "Do your best, always." On the other side, we explained, "We'll practice immediacy—if something isn't sitting right with us, we'll address it straightaway," "We'll tell the truth, always," and, "We'll give you credit when you've done a great job."

It was a beautiful way to set the scene and show new employees how important our culture was to us. It also sent a clear message that we expected our people to play an active part in keeping it alive.

> When we are surrounded by people who believe what we believe ... we're more willing to explore, and go somewhere that no one has ever gone before ...
>
> **SIMON SINEK**

One crucial tactic in building an amazing culture has been to encourage our team to think as if they own the business. We've tried to empower them to make decisions independently, but more important, we've trained the managers to let them. This is harder than it looks! A lot of managers want to hold on to control for lots of reasons. Perhaps it's fragility of ego or a lack of self-esteem that makes them want to get the credit, or perhaps they deeply care and just don't want things to go wrong.

A crucial part of having your team think like owners is to make sure the entrepreneurial spirit is kept alive, no matter how big you get. This means encouraging everyone to put forward their ideas and trying to be nimble when making decisions.

The entrepreneurial spirit has to come from the top. Whoever's at the top needs to walk around saying, "We can do better," "We don't need a meeting for that," and "Can you think of a better way?" It's this person's job to help everyone think like entrepreneurs, thereby triggering a more responsive and innovative culture.

When it comes to designing a great culture that makes people want to stick around, here are my golden rules.

GIVE CREDIT WHERE CREDIT'S DUE. Our members will often reach out to me and say, "Thanks so much for the latest edition of your magazine, *Latte*. I loved it!" or "Thanks for organizing that event with Nicole Kidman!" I'm quick to tell them that I had absolutely nothing to do with any of it; I see the magazine for the first time long after our members see it, and I wouldn't know how to run an event to save myself. I'll always be sure to direct the praise to the exceptional people who made it happen.

SAY THANKS. Sometimes just sticking a Post-it Note on a team member's desk with a "You're the best," or "I so love having you on the team," works as well as the food that any private chef could create. Buying coffee for the whole team every now and then, or sending a bunch of flowers or a card to someone who's done a great job, will always go a long way toward showing your team you've noticed them.

INVEST IN YOUR MANAGERS. If you're leading a team or running your own business, you can't do it on your own. Your managers often have a tough gig because they're managing up and managing down. Make sure you give them the time they need, the resources they're asking for, and the inspiration to get better each day. If you need any more convincing, remember that people leave managers, not companies.

ALLOW PEOPLE TO MANAGE UP. I crave people around me who are going to be real. I've watched so many speakers and celebrities over the years who have people around them who only tell them what they want to hear. In my case, I want to do better and be better, and I love when people disagree with me. It's hard to hear at first, of course, and you have to know when to take advice or discard it, but I appreciate hearing different perspectives and occasionally being told what to do.

DON'T OVERPROTECT. I watch too many managers overprotect their people, which limits learning opportunities. In the same way that children can be over-parented, the same can happen with over-managed team members. Not allowing people the space to trip up and discover what works for them as individuals can limit creativity and ultimately stunt an employee's growth.

LET PEOPLE FAIL, BUT MAKE SURE THEY LEARN. My people know they have permission to wing it and fail successfully. Failing successfully means you must admit you've failed, you must be willing to talk about it, and you must be open to learning from it.

DON'T COUNT THE HOURS. I've found that the more generous I am, the more generous my team members are in return. If a team member has to go to the doctor, don't expect them to make up the hour they missed. If there's trust between people and their managers, no one should be keeping score. If your culture is healthy and your people are engaged, it will all equal out.

LET YOUR PEOPLE WORK OUT HOW TO ACHIEVE THEIR OUT-COMES. From the outset, be really clear about your expectations of what you need from your people. We ask our team members to go away and set their own KPIs (key performance indicators), and then bring those back so we can consult on them together. I never dictate how my team members should reach their goals. I'm only interested in if the goals are achieved. Let their creativity flourish—your people will love that you trust them. Allow them to express themselves and just get on with it.

REVIEW OFTEN. Most people dread the annual performance review. So, break it down and review a little more regularly. These one-on-one sessions, even just three times a year, reveal issues more quickly, rather than waiting to hear them at review time. It also keeps motivation up when you show people you're watching and noticing their achievements along the way.

PRACTICE IMMEDIACY. If you're unhappy about something, talk about it now. Don't wait until the "right time" to address it. This will only build resentment between you and your team.

PICK UP THE BROOM. I've always tried to lead by example, and that often means rolling up my sleeves and helping to do the things that might not always fit inside the box of my job description. I want to show my team that you're never too senior to pick up a broom. There's no job in my company that I haven't done and wouldn't do again. When the business needs to rally to get a task or project done, I'll jump in and hustle every bit as hard as the next person.

LET THEM LEAVE. I'm proud that in our fourteen years of Business Chicks, we've had six people do an initial stint in the business, leave for a bit, and then come back again. I encourage people to move on when they feel the time is right. Sometimes you outgrow a role or a business and there's no point in staying there feeling stagnant. I've encouraged some top talent to go spread their wings, and it's liberating for everyone. It's even better when, after growing and developing some more skills, they come back looking for the next opportunity.

BE VULNERABLE, ALWAYS. Being a strong leader means admitting you don't have the answers, and it means owning your mistakes. It means being emotionally available for your people and holding a space for them to be vulnerable with you too.

LEADERSHIP IS ACTION, NOT POSITION. I expect leadership from everyone, not just the senior people in my company. Leadership can be as easy as being the first person to jump up and greet someone who has walked into the office. It's being the first person on the dance floor at the company holiday party. Leadership is about not assuming someone else will do it first. It's taking initiative and getting into action.

Doing what you're good at each day makes the day fly

One of the best pieces of advice I ever received is to find out what you're best at, and spend the majority of your time focused on doing just that. It's fruitless to turn your weaknesses into strengths. If you're not good at something, accept it, move on, and concentrate on amplifying your unique abilities and skills. If you're engaged in work that energizes you and that you're innately good at, you'll be in flow and you'll get real results.

Over the years, I've become obsessed with strengths-based methodology. I first learned about it probably a decade ago, and the science and research made so much sense to me.

As a basic premise, strengths-based thinking is all about working to your strengths and not spending time on the things you're not good at. When you were a kid and you came home with an A+ in English and a B- in math on your report card, your parents would likely say, "You've got to work harder on your math!" Right? I know as a parent it's tempting to have this point of view, but strengths-based thinking adopts a different perspective, which, if used correctly, would have you say, "You're good at English, so let's focus your efforts there on becoming even better at that, because it's innately where your talents lie."

Unfortunately, we can't really control the education our kids receive. There'd be a lot of upset teachers if our children walked into classrooms across the country saying, "But my parents told me it's cool for me to stop doing math." Obviously, it's different in the game of business, and if we get our people focused on what they do best, day in and day out, they'll enjoy their work so much more.

I've always been able to see the big picture very clearly, but I've never quite known how to break it down into smaller chunks and devise a plan to get us there. That's where people like my general manager, Amber, come into their own. She has "Arranger" in her top five strengths, so she loves being able to sit down and create order and process to make sure my vision is realized. Meanwhile, I'm either sitting in the corner yawning, or I've left the room altogether to dream up some new crazy idea. It's a perfect match!

When discussing people problems with the leaders in my business, I'll hear them out with their frustrations and regularly find myself saying in response, "That's because you've got them doing something they suck at. They're never going to be good at it, so it's a waste of everybody's time to get them to do it."

When faced with that dilemma, we've gone so far as to create jobs around a person's strengths (if viable for the business) that were different than the one they initially applied for.

Now we all know that you can't necessarily design your absolute dream job working every waking minute on the tasks you love doing, but by spending the majority of your time working to your strengths, it all starts to feel so much easier.

YOU WON'T PLEASE EVERYONE

A leader takes people where they would never go alone

Leadership is about leaving your ego at the door. It's about walking next to your people and saying, "We're in this together, and we're going to be fine." It's about being vulnerable enough to admit you don't have the answers, but brave enough to say the things that others are too scared to say. And none of that is easy to do.

Adults are just kids in bigger clothes with a few more filters but the same set of problems. Adults can be unpredictable and needy, and as a leader, it's your job to soothe their woes, encourage them into performance, and be there for them when you'd rather be getting your own work done—or going home when it's still light outside.

Take comfort, though. If great leadership were easy, everyone would be doing it. I don't have an MBA, but I have spent my life in the leadership trenches, and here's what I've discovered about building teams and inspiring others into action.

> ## If you want to make everyone happy, don't be a leader—sell ice cream.
> ### STEVE JOBS

YOU'LL HAVE TO PUSH THE BOUNDARIES. It's a leader's job to help their people see possibility. Sometimes that doesn't make you popular, but it'll sure as hell get things done. One time I didn't win any popularity contests was when I called the team to stretch harder at a time when they were already stretched. We'd already taken on a big task with bringing Seth Godin to Australia. Over two days, he'd present to crowds of over 6,000 people in Sydney and Melbourne at four different events.

I had been speaking with another of my idols, Arianna Huffington, for many years, and we just hadn't been able to find the space to work together. Still, I persisted (gently) until one day, an email hit my inbox. Arianna told me she'd be coming to Australia finally and asked if I'd like to have dinner. I told her that dinner would be lovely, but that I'd prefer to put her to work! And so began the negotiations between her team and mine to make it happen. When we were finally offered the two dates for her appearances, I didn't know whether to laugh or cry. They were the exact same two dates as our four events with Seth.

I knew the team was already at capacity, but I also knew that this could be done. It had to be. I just had to find a way to encourage them to see the possibility in it. Sheepishly, I went into the office the next day to break the news. Their reaction was similar to mine—I could see half of them wanting to break into tears, and the other half couldn't wipe the smiles off their faces. Luckily, my head of events, Rebecca Summers, led the way with, "Wow! Okay, this is great! We'll make it happen, Em. We'll find a way. We just have to!" Bec and I have worked together for close to a decade, so she knows better than to say no to my crazy ideas if I truly have my heart set on something. Of course, she challenges me regularly, but when it's only hard work standing in the way of achieving something, she knows to somehow find a way.

Pulling off six events over two days across two cities for over 9,000 people is not something I'd recommend for your blood pressure, but it was possibly the most alive I've ever felt. We called in the troops to help execute: ex-employees that we begged to come back and help, and any willing family members too. I flew back and forth between Sydney and Melbourne multiple times over the forty-eight hours. I was also eleven weeks pregnant with my fourth child, but I hadn't told anyone yet, so I was quietly battling nausea and ridiculous levels of tiredness. I pushed through and got it done because that's what leaders do. If I expected a stretch of my people, I'd have to stretch too.

At one of the lunches, I decided on a whim that I'd announce my pregnancy. I walked onstage and said what I needed to say, congratulating my team for the exceptional way in which they'd banded together and made the seemingly impossible possible and threw in a little, "By the way, I'm expecting, and it's such a relief to tell you all because now I can stop holding my stomach in!" I watched as my assistant, Britt, went white in the face (she couldn't believe I'd kept it from her for that long). I live for a surprise.

YOUR JOB IS TO ASK, NOT TELL. Your leadership journey never truly ends, and one thing's for sure: you're going to mess up many times over. I certainly have.

As a leader, it's critical to help team members discover their own answers to the questions on their minds. When someone asks me directly what they should do in a situation, I'll never tell them (even if the answer is really obvious to me). Instead I ask, "What do you think you should do?" I've never seen it as my responsibility as a leader to tell someone what to do. On most occasions, it's actually quite disempowering to deliver a solution to someone without encouraging some gentle introspection from them.

COURAGE AND CALMNESS IN A CRISIS ARE PARAMOUNT. In the face of what could be a crisis, leadership is having people gain confidence by the way you're handling yourself. I've always found that if you're calm and in control, you allow your team to be calm and in control too.

There have been plenty of times when we've messed up and things haven't gone our way. Once we forgot to apply for a visa for an international guest speaker and had to delay her flights out of the US by a day. Another time, just before an event, we found out a new events registration system had failed us, meaning that 600 out of our 1,400 guests would have nowhere to sit when they arrived at one of our events about fifty minutes later.

When I learned about these mistakes, I set the tone by being calm and collected, knowing that my people were looking to me for leadership.

You can always find a way to fix the mistakes you've made, but you never get a chance to take back the way you behaved. Make yourself and your team proud. Some of our best times as a team have been when we've seriously messed up and been able to sit back at the end of the day and have a big laugh at ourselves—together. Camaraderie and memories are built through shared mistakes.

YOU'LL HAVE TO MAKE TOUGH CALLS. I've never been a micromanager. I'm committed to excellence, and I may push people by saying, "We can do better," but I always let my people do their jobs. In most cases, I've been rewarded with the most wonderful people who care deeply and want to serve to the best of their abilities.

However, there are instances when people let you down, and you know in your heart that the time has come for them to move on. While it's always hard at the time to manage their exit, it's crucial for the rest of your people that you show leadership here.

We once had a team member who was exceptional. She was enthusiastic, passionate, ruthless at negotiating, and one of our highest billers. This woman was a brilliant ambassador for the business, and possibly the hardest worker I'd ever employed. Problem was, her direct style often had others in tears and she could be very difficult to work with. We tried every conceivable measure to fix the problem, but nothing worked. While she was a huge asset to the business, her methods continued to negatively impact many of the other team members, so I had to make the difficult decision to let her go.

Of course, I was worried about what the rest of the business would think of my decision, but I needn't have been. Because I decided to let her go, my team gained more respect for me and the tough call I'd made.

YOUR JOB IS TO SERVE. In my eyes, there's nothing more important than serving others, and my team members are at the very top of this list. I was putting my team members first long before I'd heard the term "servant leadership," which flips the idea that employees are meant to serve their bosses.

Servant leaders know that their people can achieve a lot when they're inspired by a purpose bigger than themselves, and they see it as their job to provide that inspiration. Servant leaders have a plan, but are nimble enough to wing it when they feel that plan isn't going to cut it anymore. They can be spontaneous when required, once they've earned the respect of their people enough for them to trust that spontaneity.

"Smile. It confuses people."

SANDI THOM

Servant leaders have a mindset of "I don't always know the way, but follow me and we'll work it out together." They're humble in their approach, they gently hold others to account, and they're kind and compassionate humans. And when it comes down to it, this is what brilliant leadership is all about.

DON'T FORGET TO LAUGH

We're taking this business thing far too seriously. I know there's a lot riding on it, but really, it's not all there is to life. It's a moment in time, a way to fill our days (and some nights), and it's undoubtedly important. What's equally important, though, is to enjoy ourselves and not take everything so seriously.

It's said that, on average, a child laughs 400 times a day. This drops to fifteen times a day by the time we're thirty-five. Imagine if we made it our job to lift this number in our workplaces? I think you'd find a whole lot more engaged people and more happy customers as a result.

Business doesn't have to be boring, but it can be because most people think that being fun is being unprofessional. Not so. It's entirely possible for you to bring your personality to your job and remain professional at the same time.

Professional does not have to mean serious. Some of the highest performing companies in the world have fun as a core value, and their customers feel this. Southwest Airlines is renowned for creating experiences that get talked about for all the right reasons. There was a video that went viral of a flight attendant reading out the safety guide, which was funnier than a stand-up comedy act. "Position your seatbelt low and tight across your hips, like my grandmother wears her support bra," she starts off saying, before continuing, "Everybody gets a door prize in the seat back in front of you, along with dirty diapers, chewing-gum wrappers, and all the other gifts you leave for us from time to time." You can hear the whole cabin cracking up as she continues with, "And if you're traveling with small children—we're sorry."

I've always tried to make our workplace fun. I'll often hide under my desk if I think someone's looking for me, and when they get close, I'll jump out and scare them. In the early days of my recruitment business, when we had to make cold calls, I'd bring in oversized sunglasses and stand up and wear them while I was phoning prospects.

I went through a phase at Business Chicks of folding the edges of the office toilet paper into triangles like they do in hotels, and for weeks no one had any idea who it was. Every time someone would use the bathroom, they'd come out saying, "Who keeps folding the toilet paper like that?" It took them ages to figure out it was me.

I'll be the person who tells people I love them and punctuates my emails with exclamation points and jokes. I'm partial to spontaneous dancing on the office desk from time to time. If an invite to a fancy dress party lands on my desk, I'm the first to RSVP. Who says life has to be boring, and who says you have to fit in? I want to light up a room, I want to have an impact on people, and I want to spread love and make a difference. Business can be an excellent vehicle for this.

We love turning everything into a game at Business Chicks. You'll often hear one of the team say, "Right, let's get out the whiteboard!" and before we know it, there are a couple of columns drawn up and two teams pegged against each other. Whenever one team gets a win, they color in a space on the column and the team with the highest bar wins. A little competition never hurt anyone.

As with everything to do with leadership and culture, it all starts at the top, so show your team you want to have fun as much as they do.

Here are some nominally boring things you can make fun.

TITLES. When I first started Business Chicks, I was called the "Chief Chick," which was fun at the time. My husband even had business cards printed up that said "Handbag to the Chief Chick," which always got the laughs. If you're in strategy, could you be "Thinker of

Deep Thoughts"? Perhaps as the office manager, you could choose "Maestro of Mayhem."

BUSINESS CARDS. There's no rule that says business cards have to be boring, but as someone who has run a large network for over a decade and collected a ton of them, I can tell you that 99 percent of them are. I've always thought that business cards are a great opportunity to convey your personality and leave people with a sense of who you are. For years, we had our coffee orders on our business cards, and I've lost count of the number of meetings I'd arrive at to find a latte sitting there waiting for me. These are just cute little conversation starters that also go a long way toward revealing who we are as people and that we don't take ourselves too seriously.

AUTO-REPLIES. Another way you can inject some more personality is to give some thought and humor to your out-of-office messages. Zoë Foster Blake's are legendary. Once I emailed her and got this back: "Today's horoscope: You will receive an annoying auto-reply from someone. Do not expect to hear from them until Monday, because that's how the planets want it and they always know what's up. Also, you will reconnect with your childhood sweetheart, eat some suspicious ham, and run for mayor. But mostly the Monday thing." Compare this brilliance with most of the inane out-of-office messages we receive each day, and you'll see which one stands out and gets remembered.

If you're given the choice, don't play it safe

We produce a conference each year, and the theme of the final night's gala event is always a hotly contested topic for our team. I'll always suggest the wackiest theme I can think of. It's way more fun to get people out of their comfort zones and do something they may not have done before. At our first conference, the theme was the movie *Priscilla, Queen of the Desert*. All of our members went to so much effort with their outfits and makeup, and it was an unforgettable experience. We flew in three drag queens, and I even dressed my three-month-old son up in a pretty pink dress because I didn't want him to miss out on the fun.

I'm always looking for ways to create more memories for my team. I remember the first time we heard that Jamie Oliver was going to speak for Business Chicks. After I hung up the phone with his people, I went straight into the supermarket and bought every single Jamie Oliver product I could get my hands on, from spatulas to spaghetti sauce. I took them all into the office and set them up with a big tablecloth over the top and invited the whole team into the boardroom. Excitedly, I asked them, "Guess who our next speaker is?" and then ripped off the cover. There were squeals of delight, and it was so much more exciting than just sending an email around.

In my early days of the recruitment business, the way we showed our people that we appreciated them was to take them out of the office for a bit of fun. We'd take them away for team-building trips to places like Queenstown in New Zealand, Nouméa in New Caledonia, and the Whitsunday Islands in Queensland a couple of times too.

The thing about these team-building weekends was that they were always a surprise. We never told the team where they were going. For some, this was an amazing adventure, and for others it sent them into a cold sweat, not knowing what to pack or what to wear. We always gave them guidelines, but many wanted more information and to feel in control.

The time we took the team to Nouméa was tricky because we needed to have everyone's passports, and I didn't want anyone to know that we were taking them overseas. I went about contacting all of the employees' families, partners, and roommates so they could hand over their passports to me, and I swore these people to secrecy. Imagine the team's shock that morning when they were bundled into minivans and escorted to the airport. There was a twist, though: I had instructed the drivers to go via the domestic airport first, to throw the team off the scent. Everyone was jumping up and down when we got there, only to get even more excited when the vans kept moving through the domestic airport and on to the international airport. It was pretty special to watch.

At first, there was never really an agenda apart from saying thank you to our team members, but as the company grew, we started implementing more structured activities that would benefit the business when we got back to the office. The objective was always the same, though: have fun, get to know one another, and make everyone feel appreciated.

Nobody looks stupid when they're having fun.

AMY POEHLER

A lot of business owners will be quick to tell you they just can't afford to do this for their team. I'd say that (especially in the early days) you can't afford not to. Your employees will go on to tell everyone they know about your generosity, and it will help you build an employer brand that outsmarts your competitors.

And who knows? You just might have a heap of fun along the way too.

OVER TO YOU

"After the 2004 federal election in Canada, my former boss, the Deputy Prime Minister of Canada, and I met with a journalist who challenged us to climb Mount Kilimanjaro to raise money for charity. We accepted the challenge, and that was the beginning of my fly-by-the-seat-of-my-pants path. The day after I summited Kili I decided to pay a visit to Uganda, where I had been born but had no allegiance to, or memory of. After being there a few days, I returned to Canada, and gave notice at my job because I felt compelled to work in service to underserved populations in the developing world. Six months later, I found myself in the driving seat navigating unknown territory creating a foundation for a high-profile, Canadian female philanthropist. That mission eventually led to me risking it all with no money and no safety net and starting G(irls)20, and that led me to the helm of the Malala Fund. I have spent the last fifteen years working in service to girls and women, in large part because this 5-foot, 1.25-inch former refugee said yes to a physical challenge I never thought would put me on top of so many mountains and standing on so many ledges."

FARAH MOHAMED
Former CEO, Malala Fund, and Founder, G(irls)20

SPEAK UP

Every day, you have the power to choose our better history—by opening your hearts and minds, by speaking up for what you know is right.

MICHELLE OBAMA

The advantage of only ever having worked for myself (apart from that casual job I had while I was at school) is that I've been able to choose who I hang out with each day. Given the chance, I'm always going to choose people who are self-aware, are progressive, and believe in fairness and equity in all their forms. My unique situation has meant I've never had to spend any meaningful time with racist or homophobic people, for example. It also means that I've been sheltered from many of the realities of gender bias, discrimination, and harassment. Sadly, though, no one is immune, and I've certainly had my share of experiences that have shaped how I view the world and the impact I want to make. I'm also in the position of hearing hundreds of stories from our members each year and consulting with our corporate partners to help move the needle on gender issues.

Many years ago, we won a business award. We were a small team back then and, perhaps unsurprisingly, only one of us was a man. When our name was called out, the whole team went up to accept the award. There was a well-known media identity emceeing the event. He shook our hands and congratulated us. I'd met this man on the set of television shows several times, so we knew each other well enough to have a little bit of friendly banter onstage, but what happened next floored us all.

He made a joke about all these attractive women (cringe) and the one man who got to work with us. Then he went on to say, "So, Em, what does this lucky man get to do in your company each day?" Put on the spot with an irrelevant question, in a room of a thousand people, and

"We cannot succeed when half
of us are held back."

MALALA YOUSAFZAI

with a microphone thrust in my face, I explained that he was in finance. The emcee threw his head back and laughed loudly, "Ah, typical! The man looks after the money!"

Whatever elation we had all felt disappeared and was replaced by shock. We felt belittled, and I felt disappointed in myself for not having the guts to respond with something like, "Yeah, but the women in my company make the money!"

From that moment on, I vowed to take a stand and call out comments like these whenever they were made. I hadn't been prepared then, but I sure as heck would be in the future, no matter how big or small the remark. The impact these offhand messages send are felt, and they matter.

They need to stop.

Here's a very simple example for you. An email hit my inbox once from a new organic e-commerce site, so I clicked through, downloaded the app, and took a look around. It looked good—good design, good layout, good navigation. Then I got to a category called "Moms." Intrigued, I clicked through, and you guessed it: it was full of diapers, baby supplies, baby food, and related products. I looked for a section called "Dads" and couldn't find anything.

I took a deep breath, found the customer service button and typed:

Hey team,

Just downloaded the app—congrats, it looks great!—but wanted to pass on the first thing that struck me. Under "Moms" you've got diapers and other great baby-related products, but are these products only for moms? Do fathers not change diapers too? Is parenting only a mother's responsibility?

The messaging is subtle, of course, but that's exactly what unconscious bias is—subtle and not intentionally discriminate.

I'm really, really disappointed to see this. Can't help but think you've just sent women back about thirty years and would love to hear your thoughts.

Warmest wishes,
Emma Isaacs

I waited for their response. Nothing. It's now been well over a year and I'm still waiting. Imagine, though, if fifty, or a hundred, or five-hundred people wrote a similar email? They may just sit up and listen.

I recently gave a speech after which the organizer opened the floor to questions. A young woman told me that she often experienced unconscious bias bordering on gender discrimination in her workplace, and asked me what she should do about it. My advice was to call it out, and take a bullet for all the women behind her.

There are ways to explain to people that gender bias, unconscious or not, can't be tolerated if we're to get ahead. I think a good way to start is to take an unemotional approach. While you have a right to be angry, approaching the conversation from an indignant place will only alienate your audience.

The young woman said if she were to speak out against the discrimination she was experiencing, it would make it hard to continue to show up to work each day. I acknowledged her predicament, but also said that if nothing changes, nothing changes.

I feel we all have a responsibility to do our bit when it comes to stamping out bias. It's not just up to the leaders or people in the public eye to police this—it must come from everyone. And if this young woman's workplace wasn't willing to address it, perhaps it was time for her to move on and find one that did.

For any industry to thrive, we need more equity, and we need people calling out unconscious bias. We've got work to do here, and that work belongs to all of us. A lot of the time, it's systemic and covert, and people are just unaware that they're perpetuating the biases.

I was looking at properties online recently, and one caught my attention for all the wrong reasons. The headline of the advertisement read, "Your very own private paradise—perfect for a businessman or celebrity." Immediately, I saw red. Why couldn't a businesswoman own it? Why must it only be available to a businessman?

I sat down and crafted an email to the agent, pointing out how his choice of words ruled women out of this opportunity. Always trying to see the best in every person and situation, I acknowledged that I was sure he hadn't meant it, but I asked him to rectify the wording of the ad regardless.

The poor bloke responded the next day, apologizing for the oversight. He said he'd been writing that term "businessman" for most properties with a high price tag for as long as he could remember. It had never even occurred to him to write anything else, but he would in the future. Before I replied, I checked the advertisement again and smiled to see "businessman" had been replaced with "businessperson." You've got to take the little wins.

This topic deserves a whole book on its own, but from working in this space for over a decade now, I can give you a snapshot of what I know. While we can impact and influence the system to a point (calling out the discrimination, not accepting harassment, educating others about unconscious bias, etc.) systemic, real change takes time. Movements like Me Too and Time's Up help keep the issue in the spotlight (where it belongs), but there's no one quick fix or silver bullet. It's going to take every one of us to engage in constructive, open dialogue and not stop until we finally exist in a world where our workplaces are equal. It has to come from all angles, be it one Hollywood actress publicly calling out how she was paid less than her male costar (or worse, harassed), or an early morning confrontation between a husband and wife about why he feels he should go to work and she should stay home with the unexpected sick child. We've got to believe we're getting there.

And while we're getting there, it seems to me it's the responsibility of all of us to lift our voices and be heard, no matter what it takes.

We owe it to the next woman to call this stuff out. We owe it to our sisters and our daughters. We owe it to our mothers, who most likely experienced far more of it than we ever will. And, most critically, we owe it to ourselves.

SUPPORT, DON'T COMPETE

Women don't need to walk over each other to get ahead. Those days have passed, and it's time for a different conversation. Instead of competing with each other, we must fiercely compete with ourselves and get obsessed with how to keep getting better.

At the Australian Open tennis tournament in 2017, Serena Williams bravely defeated her older sister Venus in straight sets. This was her twenty-third Grand Slam title, and at the time, it made her the oldest Grand Slam champion in history at the age of thirty-five. She also happened to be pregnant.

In her speech, Venus honored her younger sister, saying, "Your win has always been my win." You could almost hear the sisterhood erupt into a collective cheer. It's a beautiful sound that I've been privileged to hear throughout my career many a time, and I'm always the one cheering the loudest.

Jealousy has never made sense to me. Just like guilt, jealousy is an emotion that eats you up and holds you back. You bought a new property? Great! You got a big promotion? Awesome news. You deserve it! You're pregnant? Amazing. You'll be the best mom!

I often get asked how we can support each other and make the sisterhood even stronger, and I always say that it starts with the individual. Yes, we're powerful en masse, but tuning in to your own feelings and how you react to another woman's successes can often be just as powerful.

If you feel a pang of jealousy when you see another woman buy the house of her dreams, or cringe when a woman gets pregnant while you're struggling to, I encourage you to meditate on these feelings for a second. It's not to take away the pain that you haven't bought your dream home yet or to minimize your fertility or relationship issues. That pain is very, very real, but we cannot control what happens outside of us. We must learn to accept it, celebrate all women's achievements, and watch our own self-talk and thinking.

Invest in women

I get excited thinking about the possibilities we can create together for women. I've spent the last decade of my life serving women—a mentoring session here, providing some angel investment funding there, and connecting people who'd benefit from the introduction. Although it's largely invisible work, it's also really important, and we can all contribute to it.

We need women building and controlling their own profitable businesses. We need women around boardroom tables across the globe making decisions and having their voices heard. We need women speaking up and taking more risks. And we all need to be playing a part in backing not only ourselves, but also each other, to make this happen.

I believe that investing in women (no matter how much or how little) is the solution to so many problems across the world. When we invest in women, we invest in communities, and that's an investment in the future. A report from the 2009 Clinton Global Initiative says that when women work, they invest 90 percent of their income back into their families, compared to 35 percent for men. When we invest in women, we solve myriad problems, ranging from lifting communities out of poverty to tackling the inequity in venture capital. I feel strongly that it's the responsibility of all of us to back other women and support them where we can.

Everyone has a different level of resources available to them, but it's going to take us all tapping into the resources we *do* have to even out the playing field. If it's time you have, then give that to mentor a young woman. If you've got skills or knowledge, share them where you can. If it's money, then offer that. You might not have the amount needed to access equity in a start-up, but maybe you could donate to organizations like The Hunger Project or Kiva, both of which have brilliant funding models for getting women off the ground in their own businesses and helping them expand their ventures through donations or microloans. One of our much-loved members, Justine, bought one hundred Business Chicks memberships last year and asked us to find women who could use the leg up, creating the most beautiful of ripple effects.

My CEO in Australia sits on a charity board to lend her expertise and networks. Business Chicks member Shelly Horton started "walk and talks" to help mentor other women. There are ways!

I also believe we've got to back our friends no matter what. Enthusiastically like and share their social posts. Unashamedly talk to anyone who'll listen about their achievements. Buy their products, and don't ask for them for free. Attend their events, and bring a friend or two. Endorse their brands. This is what friends do, and this is how the sisterhood is built, one act of encouragement at a time.

EVERYONE IS WINGING IT

Two days before I sent this book off to my publishers, on a whim, I emailed a bunch of dear friends asking them if they'd ever winged it. My inbox blew up. Turns out, we're all doing it, yet we fall prey to thinking that everyone else is in full control and knows exactly what they're doing.

My friend Jules told me about the time she was asked to audition as an on-camera host for MTV just five weeks after she had her first baby. "I had never auditioned for anything like it before and had no idea how to 'be on TV,' but I thought, 'What the heck? I'll just wing it,'" she said. "I went home that afternoon thinking, 'Ahhh, that was a nice afternoon out of the house—I'll just go back to my normal life now,' but I got a call a week later from MTV letting me know I landed the job." Jules spent the next three months traveling around Australia, tiny baby in tow, and has never looked back.

Author and speaker Janine Shepherd reminded me how she learned to fly airplanes after doctors told her she'd never walk again. One of my team members, Cecelia, told me about the time she redesigned a website that receives hundreds of thousands of clicks a day. "I had not designed a website in almost ten years, since I left university, but I said, 'Sure, I'll give it a go,' and then I had a panic attack at my desk."

I loved the story Shelley Sullivan sent me. Shelley is the founder of international beauty brand ModelCo. Shelley started out her career as a model agent, always taking the time to really listen to what her models were saying. She'd hear them rave about the products they loved and dream about the ones they wished existed. "I was also looking at the way they applied makeup and tanning products, and from there, I was inspired to first create a heated eyelash curler," says Shelley. "At the time I launched LASHWAND Heated Eyelash Curler, there were no other unique, innovative, solution-focused beauty products on the market. So I saw a gap and went for it."

This was new territory not only for Shelley, but also for the market. When she first started out, her innovation was a pet project. She had no idea that ModelCo would go on to become the beauty juggernaut it is today. "I saw an opportunity and took the plunge," Shelley says. "I didn't know anything about beauty products. I had two choices: stick to what's safe, or risk on innovation. I chose innovation."

Shelley acknowledges this is the reason behind ModelCo's sixteen-year success story. "Committing to innovation became the backbone of our success, and it still is today. My experience has always been that the market will generally forgive you for making mistakes, but it won't forgive you for standing still."

The hard stuff is the best stuff

When my world was crashing down in the first year of moving to the US, there were times when I wondered whether I was cut out for the challenge. There were times when it would have been easier for me to admit defeat and return home to Australia.

And it was at those times I had to remind myself that the hard stuff is usually the best stuff, and if it were too easy, I'd probably be bored anyway.

In the times I couldn't figure out which way to turn with the American business, I got busy innovating elsewhere. I threw myself into being as useful as I could with the Australian business, creating new products, and also looking at how I could dial up other revenue sources. I turned a house into an Airbnb property, learning all I could about that system and trying to make the experience as amazing as possible for our guests. I loved the challenge and have since replicated the success with a few more Airbnb properties here in Los Angeles. And just recently we've bought a fixer-upper house that we're flipping because, well, one should never stand still, right?

Four years ago, could I have imagined that I'd have been back and forth between Australia and the US more than thirty times, that I'd have another baby, and that my kids would have convincing American accents? Probably not, but that's what winging it is all about. It's the doing despite the not knowing. And in many ways, being away has given us so many benefits. I've gained enormous perspective. Decisions in the Australian business seem much easier to make from afar—it's like I can see exactly what needs to be done. I've also learned a ton by seeing firsthand how American businesses grow and the sheer velocity with which it happens.

> When you believe that you can turn your hand to anything or you know in your heart you have a strong work ethic, winging it doesn't seem so scary and is often the best boot up the bum to just f***ing do it!
>
> **MICHELLE BRIDGES**

Sometimes, you really do have to take a step back in order to take a step forward. Now that I've experienced having the wind knocked out of me and catching my breath again, I've attacked our business opportunity in the US from a completely different angle, and there's no stopping me. I'm armed with a long list of what worked and what didn't, and even though it sucked going through the angst and pain of failing, I'm tremendously grateful for the lessons.

Facebook founder Mark Zuckerberg once said, "Move fast and break things," and I almost cried because of the resonance I felt with those words. To me, these words said, "Just get on with it. Make mistakes. Fail quickly. Get going." I fell so deeply in love with the sentiment of this quote that I asked the team to call our annual conference "Movers and Breakers" because I felt that's exactly what we'd been encouraging women to do for so many years.

Truly entrepreneurial people learn through the doing and through the moving and breaking, not the thinking. They build the plane while it's flying. While other people are still thinking of the idea, they've tried ten different versions, discarded nine of them, and became obsessed with making the final time different.

These people are winging it. They're the pilots of their own lives. They have their heads in the clouds and their hands firmly on the controls.

MAKE YOUR MOVE

I want you to say yes to things. I want you to move at a speed that makes you feel alive. I want you to give more attention to your first waking thoughts each day and run toward the ideas that make you sit a little more upright. Bring back a little more recklessness: go with what feels good and right, not what might work because you've tried it before and it sort of worked.

Instead, try new things! Make mistakes! Experiment! Laugh at yourself! Imagine "What if?" Shout "Pick me!" Jump in. Help each other. Have a try even when you don't know how. Be the first one on the dance floor. Smile at strangers. Fail epically. Ask dumb questions. Say no to negativity. Try again. Don't overthink.

What I hope this book does is remind you that we've all got fight in us and that if we band together (now that you know we're all in the same boat, winging it every day), there'll be a cumulative force to cheer you on. I hope it inspires you to know you're not alone and nudges you an inch (wait, a mile!) toward your goals.

If you take just one idea away from this book, it should be that you are in the driver's seat. You get to choose. You call the shots. You get to go create anything you want. There's a magic in that, but it comes with two caveats: you must start somewhere, and you're the only one who can make it happen.

So what are you waiting for?

SPECIAL PEOPLE

Writing this book was definitely one of the hardest things I've ever done. It was a lot of hours trying to sit still (not my forte) and having others coerce me into concentrating at every available moment.

I owe this gentle convincing in the most part to Lucy Ormonde, who gets the award for being the only person who was able to make me do so until the end. Apart from being a superior editor and project manager, she often worked under pressure-cooker conditions during her visits to Los Angeles (aka the Isaacs household) and coped beautifully—thrived even! I'm sure she'll tell you that working with me on this book was worse than herding cats (which she's never been asked to do before either). Through various techniques—threats, rewards, encouragement, and hundreds of cups of mint tea—she assured me I was doing well, but never quite said it like that so that I always felt there was more work to do. You're 100 percent rad, Luce.

Big thanks to Milla, Honey, Indie, Ryder, and Piper for persevering with me while I got this book out, and to baby, who kicked encouragement throughout the writing of it. They wing it every day and remind me to do the same. Also to my parents, who taught me kindness—perhaps the life skill that's most underestimated but the one thing we all need more of.

And, of course, to Rowan, who creates an adventure wherever we go and is perhaps the only person who wings it more than I do.

Endless gratitude to the team at Sounds True, led fearlessly by the beautiful Diana Ventimiglia, and to my literary agent, Stacy Testa of Writers House. These two women saw something in me that many didn't and have encouraged me more than they know.

Thank you for always listening, Narelle, Tania, Maria, Hayley, Vanessa, and much gratitude also to Karina, Mariana, Callen, and Bre, who keep (and have kept) the wheels spinning.

And to Liv, Ambs, Sums, Bods, Tor, and Dani—I'm eternally indebted to you beautiful souls. For lots of stuff. And to everyone else who has helped shape Business Chicks into what it is today—you know who you are.

NOTES

Just Start

6. **"I think you must always . . ."** Brian Chesky, *Forbes*, September 28, 2017, pressreader.com/usa/forbes9g84/20170928/282286730406291.

9. **"Amazon's current market value is . . ."** Data is from "Amazon.com, Inc. Common Stock Summary Data," NASDAQ, accessed April 2018, nasdaq.com/symbol/amzn.

9. **"Bezos says that if you wait for . . ."** Details from Jeff Bezos's "2016 Letter to Shareholders," The Amazon Blog, April 12, 2017, amazon .com/p/feature/z6o9g6sysxur57l.

You Can't Control Anything Outside of You

25. **"When you believe you can . . ."** You can learn more about this concept by watching Carol Dweck's TED Talk, "The Power of Believing That You Can Improve," November 2014, ted.com /talks/carol_dweck_the_power_of_believing_that_you_can _improve?language=en.

32. **"Fear is at the root of so many . . ."** Sheryl Sandberg, *Lean In: Women, Work, and the Will to Lead* (New York: Alfred A. Knopf, 2013), 165.

33. **"Doubt kills more dreams . . ."** Suzy Kassem, *The Writings of Suzy Kassem*, suzykassem.com/wisdom of suzy kassem quotes.pdf.

36. **"In fact, the *Wall Street Journal* . . ."** Details are from "Employers Find 'Soft Skills' Like Critical Thinking in Short Supply," by Kate Davidson in the *Wall Street Journal*, August 30, 2016, wsj.com /articles/employers-find-soft-skills-like-critical-thinking-in-short -supply-1472549400.

42. **"Our deepest fear is not . . ."** Marianne Williamson, *A Return to Love: Reflections on the Principles of "A Course in Miracles"* (New York: HarperCollins, 1992).

44. **"Those photos tell a story . . ."** You can read the full post on Samantha Wills's website (samanthawillsfoundation.org/); it's called "Social

Impact: A Nomination & An Apology," dated September 30, 2017.

46. **"The woman who does not require . . ."** This quote was taken from the headline of an article written by Mohadesa Najumi, "Why the Woman Who Does Not Require Validation from Anyone Is the Most Feared Individual on the Planet," *HuffPost*, May 15, 2014, 6:59 a.m. BST, huffingtonpost.co.uk/mohadesa-najumi/ban-bossy-women -who-do-not-need-validation-are-feared_b_4971919.html.

Getting Ahead

57. **"The people who make it . . ."** Quincy Jones, *Q: The Autobiography of Quincy Jones* (New York: Three Rivers Press, 2002), 266.

60. **"Hustle beats talent . . ."** Ross Simmonds, "26 Hustle Driven Quotes to Get You Fired Up to Achieve Your Dreams," Ross Simmonds (website), April 24, 2018, rosssimmonds.com/hustle-quotes/.

62. **"Instead of wondering . . ."** Seth Godin, sethgodin.com.

64. **"The world has woken up to. . ."** You can watch Brené Brown's TED Talk, "The Power of Vulnerability," June 2010, at ted.com/talks /brene_brown_the_power_of_vulnerability.

66. **"There's a wise saying . . ."** Daniel Flynn, "FY17 Year in Review – Better Before Bigger: An open letter to our Thankyou Family," Thankyou Blog, December 7, 2017, thankyou.co/blog/2017/12 /fy17-year-in-review-better-before-bigger.

66. **"Warren Buffett is the world's . . ."** From "Warren Buffett," *Forbes*, accessed April 2018, forbes.com/profile /warren-buffett/#6e006eae4639.

66. **"In 2016, Charlie Munger, Buffett's business . . ."** Munger made statements at the Daily Journal Corporation annual meeting in Los Angeles on February 10, 2016, Latticework Investing (website), March 3, 2019, latticeworkinvesting.com/category /daily-journal-annual-meeting/.

69. **"Early on in my career . . ."** Zuckerberg stated this fact during Facebook Q&A on November 6, 2014, newsroom.fb.com /news/2014/11/highlights-from-qa-with-mark/.

74. **"A 2015 study conducted by . . ."** Study by Margo Hilbrecht, Bryan Smale, and Steven E. Mock, "Highway to Health? Commute Time and Well-Being Among Canadian Adults," *World Leisure Journal*, 56 (2), 2014, (November 2014): 151–163, tandfonline.com/doi/abs/10.1080 /16078055.2014.903723.

Cultivating Relationships

83. **"People will forget what you . . ."** It's difficult to pinpoint the source of this quote, but it is widely attributed to Maya Angelou. Alternatively, Carl Buehner, in a book published many years earlier, said, "They may forget what you said—but they will never forget how you made them feel." Quoted in Richard Evans's *Richard Evans' Quote Book* (Salt Lake City, UT: Publishers Press, 1971).

86. **"It's nice to be important . . ."** John Marks Templeton, *Discovering the Laws of Life* (West Conshohocken, PA: Templeton Foundation Press, 1994), 287.

95. **"One of the fundamental basics . . ."** You can learn more about neuro-linguistic programming and the creators of the theory, Richard Bandler and John Grinder, at the NLP University website, nlpu.com/NLPU.html.

Running a Business

101. **"In Australia, more than 60 percent . . ."** From Libby-Jane Charleston, "Why Small Businesses Fail in Australia," *HuffPost*, September 28, 2015, huffingtonpost.com.au/2015/09/28/small -business-failure_n_8187166.html.

101. **"In the US, 20 percent . . ."** From US Bureau of Labor Statistics, "Business Employment Dynamics: Entrepreneurship & the U.S Economy (1994–2015)," bls.gov/bdm/entrepreneurship/bdm _chart3.htm.

102. **"One of the hardest . . ."** Ziad K. Abdelnour, ziadkabdelnour.com /ziad-k-abdelnour-quotes/.

106. **"Don't find customers . . ."** Seth Godin, sethgodin.com

107. **"Alyce Tran's luxury accessories . . ."** Details about Alyce Tran are
      from "How Alyce Tran Turned a Fashion Blog into a $15 Million
      Business," by Dana McCauley, news.com.au, January 16, 2017, news.
      com.au/finance/small-business/how-alyce-tran-turned-a-fashion
      -blog-into-a-15-million-business/news-story/55ae3d21cac1263cffb59
      ab899c0d99d.

108. **"Netflix began as a DVD . . ."** Details from David Pogue, "A Stream of
      Movies, Sort of Free," *New York Times*, January 25, 2007, nytimes
      .com/2007/01/25/technology/25pogue.html.

108. **"It's now the world's leading . . ."** From Seth Fiegerman, "Netflix
      Nears 100 Million Subscribers," CNN, April 17, 2017, money.cnn
      .com/2017/04/17/technology/netflix-subscribers/index.html.

109. **"Great companies start . . ."** Guy Kawasaki, online interview with
      Forbes.com CEO Network, September 9, 2004, forbes.com
      /ceonetwork/2004/09/10/0910chat_transcript.html.

110. **"Bootstrapping means starting a business . . ."** To read more
      about bootstrapping, see Ryan Smith, "Why Every Startup Should
      Bootstrap," *Harvard Business Review* (website), March 2, 2016, hbr
      .org/2016/03/why-every-startup-should-bootstrap.

114. **"Henry Ford is contentiously credited as . . ."** From Patrick
      Vlaskovits, "Henry Ford, Innovation, and That 'Faster Horse' Quote,"
      Harvard Business Review (website), August 29, 2011, hbr.org/2011/08
      /henry-ford-never-said-the-fast.

122. **"One survey found that social . . ."** From "The QI Sprout Social
      Index," Survata, April 2016, sproutsocial.com/insights/data/q2-2016/.

126. **"I'm the one who decides . . ."** Georgio Armani in Abram Brown,
      "100 Quotes on Business From the 100 Greatest Living
      Business Minds," *Forbes*, September 19, 2017, forbes.com/sites
      /abrambrown/2017/09/19/100-quotes-on-business-from-the-100
      -greatest-business-minds/#5b807c005631.

126. **"Nasty Gal has just filed for bankruptcy . . ."** Details about Nasty Gal's
      bankruptcy from Clare O'Connor, "As Nasty Gal Files Bankruptcy,
      Founder Sophia Amoruso's Fortune Decimated,"

Forbes, November 11, 2016, forbes.com/sites/clareoconnor/2016/11/11 /as-nasty-gal-files-bankruptcy-founder-sophia-amorusos-fortune -decimated/#3cf5c11a6da8.

132. **"There will come a time . . ."** Louis L'Amour, *Lonely on the Mountain* (New York: Bantam Books, 1980), 1.

132. **"We all know Richard is forever . . ."** You can read all about Richard's projects here: "14 Virgin Companies That Even Richard Branson Could Not Stop Going Bust," *Business Insider*, May 31, 2016, businessinsider.com /richard-branson-fails-virgin-companies-that-went-bust-2016-5.

133. **"Failure is an event . . ."** Zig Ziglar, *See You at the Top* (Gretna, LA: Pelican Publishing Company, 2000), 62.

134. **"When life gets you down . . ."** Said by Dory in *Finding Nemo*, directed by Andrew Stanton (Emeryville, CA: Walt Disney Pictures and Pixar Animation Studios, 2003), DVD.

Don't Call Me Superwoman

143. **"There's an idea called the . . ."** David Sedaris wrote about this in *The New Yorker*. From "Laugh, Kookaburra: A Day in the Bush, a Night at Home," *The New Yorker*, August 17, 2009. See also: Chris Guillebeau, "The 4 Burners Theory: Choosing Between Family, Friends, Work and Health," *HuffPost*, November 17, 2011.

150. **"When something bad happens, you have . . ."** It's actually hard to pinpoint the source of this quote, but I like to think that it is the great Dr. Seuss.

Money Is Not a Dirty Word

158. **"Money is fun to make . . ."** Sara Blakely quoted in Clare O'Connor, "American Booty," *Forbes*, March 26, 2012, forbes.com /forbes/2012/0326/billionaires-12-feature-spanx-sara-blakely-retail -american-booty.html#187de9404d73.

159. **"I remember one part where . . ."** Quote from Napoleon Hill, *Think and Grow Rich* (Meriden, CT: Ralston Society, 1937).

168. **"When I bought Business Chicks . . ."** Kudos to Kids Helpline, the Australian children's charity who came up with the initial concept for Business Chicks. After I purchased the business, we maintained our partnership for many years, and I'm proud of the work and the amplification of their brand we were able to achieve together.

The People Equation

173. **"I hire people who are brighter . . ."** Lee Iacocca in Jonathan Danylko, "How to Hire the Right People to Represent Your Company," *DanylkoWeb* (blog), *Danylko Web*, January 15, 2007, danylkoweb.com /blog/how-to-hire-the-right-people-to-represent-your-company-H5.

175. **"The company's culture statement . . ."** Sheryl Sandberg's words paraphrased from Alyson Shontell, "Sheryl Sandberg: 'The Most Important Document Ever to Come out of the Valley,'" *Business Insider Australia*, February 5, 2013, businessinsider.com.au /netflixs-management-and-culture-presentation-2013-2#-1.

179. **"What they discovered were twelve . . ."** Details from Marcus Buckingham and Curt Coffman, *First Break All the Rules: What the World's Greatest Managers Do Differently* (New York: Gallup Press, 2016), 24.

180. **"When we are surrounded . . ."** See "TEDxMaastricht - Simon Sinek – 'First Why, Then Trust,'" TEDx Talks, YouTube video, April 6, 2011, 0:17:07, youtube.com/watch?v=4VdO7LuoBzM&vl=en.

184. **"Over the years, I've become obsessed . . ."** This theory originates in the field of social work. Dennis Saleebey, "The Strengths Perspective in Social Work Practice: Extensions and Cautions," *Social Work* 41 (3.1), 1996: 296–305; 'Strengths Based Models in *Social Work*,' Oxford Bibliographies, May 25, 2011.

190. **"Smile. It confuses..."** This is the debut studio album by Scottish singer Sandi Thom, released in June 2006.

191. **"There was a video that . . ."** See "Hilarious Southwest Flight Attendant," Mary Cobb Smile High Club, YouTube video, April 12, 2014, 0:03:05, youtube.com/watch?v=07LFBydGjaM.

Over to You

199. "Every day, you have the power to . . ." Michelle Obama, "Remarks from the First Lady at Topeka School District Senior Recognition Day," May 17, 2014, obamawhitehouse .archives.gov/the-press-office/2014/05/17 /remarks-first-lady-topeka-school-district-senior-recognition-day.

200. "We cannot succeed . . ." See Edith Lederer, "Malala Celebrates 16th Birthday with UN Address," July 12, 2013, apnews .com/9689f1def46148fdbea2accad4191ae2.

205. "A report from the 2009 . . ." Details from Clinton Global Initiative, "Empowering Girls & Women," 2009, un.org/en/ecosoc/phlntrpy /notes/clinton.pdf.

208. "Move fast and break things . . ." It's probably worth noting that Zuckerberg has since said the company ethos has changed to "Move fast with stable infrastructure." The original statement still resonates with me. Drake Baer, "Mark Zuckerberg Explains Why Facebook Doesn't 'Move Fast and Break Things' Anymore," *Business Insider Australia*, May 3, 2014, businessinsider.com.au /mark-zuckerberg-on-facebooks-new-motto-2014-5.

ABOUT THE AUTHOR

Emma Isaacs is the founder and global CEO of Business Chicks. Emma is a modern-day role model, proving that anything is possible for anyone wishing to strive for more in their lives and careers.

A business owner by the age of eighteen, property investor by nineteen, and millionaire by twenty-three, Emma Isaacs has entrepreneurship and achievement in her DNA. Aside from being the founder of Business Chicks—a thriving global community that operates on two continents in eleven cities, producing more than one hundred events annually, with past speakers including Sir Richard Branson, Sarah Jessica Parker, Diane von Furstenberg, Kate Hudson, and Arianna Huffington, among others—she's also a bestselling author and mother to six kids under age eleven.

Emma doesn't believe in work/life balance, preferring to advocate for a full life where people are in constant evaluation of what they truly want from it. A fearless leader with seemingly never-ending courage to spare, Emma inspires thousands with her boundless energy and ability to see possibility wherever she goes.

ABOUT SOUNDS TRUE

Sounds True is a multimedia publisher whose mission is to inspire and support personal transformation and spiritual awakening. Founded in 1985 and located in Boulder, Colorado, we work with many of the leading spiritual teachers, thinkers, healers, and visionary artists of our time. We strive with every title to preserve the essential "living wisdom" of the author or artist. It is our goal to create products that not only provide information to a reader or listener but also embody the quality of a wisdom transmission.

For those seeking genuine transformation, Sounds True is your trusted partner. At SoundsTrue.com you will find a wealth of free resources to support your journey, including exclusive weekly audio interviews, free downloads, interactive learning tools, and other special savings on all our titles.

To learn more, please visit SoundsTrue.com/freegifts or call us toll-free at 800.333.9185.